Anonymous

Hymns and Tunes

for home worship

Anonymous

Hymns and Tunes
for home worship

ISBN/EAN: 9783337291631

Printed in Europe, USA, Canada, Australia, Japan

Cover: Foto ©Lupo / pixelio.de

More available books at **www.hansebooks.com**

HYMNS AND TUNES.

Songs for Home-Worship.

GERMANY. L. M.

1. Earth has a joy unknown in heaven,—
The new-born peace of sin forgiven:
Tears of such pure and deep delight,
Ye angels! never dimmed your sight.

 Ye saw of old on chaos rise
The beauteous pillars of the skies:
Ye know where Morn exulting springs,
And Evening folds her drooping wings.

 Bright heralds of the Eternal Will,
Abroad his errands ye fulfil;
Or, throned in floods of beamy day,
Symphonious in his presence play.

 But I amid your choirs shall shine,
And all your knowledge will be mine:
Ye on your harps must lean to hear
A secret chord that mine will bear.

2. Bless, O my soul! the living God;
Call home thy thoughts that rove abroad;
Let all the powers within me join
In work and worship so divine.

 Bless, O my soul! the God of grace;
His favors claim thy highest praise:
Why should the wonders he hath wrought
Be lost in silence, and forgot?

 'Tis he, my soul, who sent his Son
To die for crimes which thou hast done;
He owns the ransom, and forgives
The hourly follies of our lives.

 Let the whole earth his power confess;
Let the whole earth adore his grace:
The Gentile with the Jew shall join
In work and worship so divine.

CHRISTMAS HYMN. 7s.   C. M. CADY.

3. Fount of everlasting love!
Rich thy streams of mercy are:
Flowing purely from above,
Beauty marks their course afar.

 Lo! thy Church, thy garden now,
Blooms beneath the heavenly shower:
Sinners feel and melt and bow;
Mild, yet mighty, is thy power.

 God of grace, before thy throne
Here our warmest thanks we bring;
Thine the glory, thine alone:
Loudest praise to thee we sing.

 Hear, oh! hear our grateful song;
Let thy Spirit still descend;
Roll the tide of grace along,
Widening, deepening, to the end.

4. Children of the heavenly King,
As ye journey, sweetly sing.—
Sing your Saviour's worthy praise,
Glorious in his works and ways.

 Ye are travelling home to God
In the way the fathers trod;
They are happy now, and ye
Soon their happiness shall see.

 Fear not, brethren; joyful stand
On the borders of your land:
Jesus Christ, your Father's Son,
Bids you undismayed go on.

 Lord, submissive make us go,
Gladly leaving all below:
Only thou our Leader be,
And we still will follow thee.

Songs for Home-Worship.

CONCORD. S. M.

5. O Lord our God! arise;
The cause of Truth maintain;
And wide o'er all the peopled world
Extend her blessed reign.

Thou Prince of life! arise,
Nor let thy glory cease:
Far spread the conquests of thy grace,
And bless the earth with peace.

Thou Holy Ghost! arise;
Extend thy healing wing;
And o'er a dark and ruined world
Let light and order spring.

O all ye nations! rise;
To God, the Saviour, sing;
From shore to shore, from earth to heaven
Let echoing anthems ring.

6. "The Lord is risen indeed:"
Now is his work performed;
Now is the mighty Captive freed,
And Death, our foe, disarmed.

"The Lord is risen indeed:"
The grave hath lost its prey:
With him is risen the ransomed seed
To reign in endless day.

"The Lord is risen indeed:"
He lives, to die no more;
He lives the sinner's cause to plead,
Whose curse and shame he bore.

"The Lord is risen indeed:"
Attending angels, hear;
Up to the courts of heaven with speed
The joyful tidings bear.

ROTHWELL. L. M.

7. Before Jehovah's awful throne,
Ye nations, bow with sacred joy:
Know that the Lord is God alone;
He can create, and he destroy.

We are his people, we his care,
Our souls and all our mortal frame:
What lasting honors shall we rear,
Almighty Maker, to thy name?

We'll crowd thy gates with thankful songs,
High as the heavens our voices raise;
And Earth, with her ten thousand tongues,
Shall fill thy courts with sounding praise.

Wide as the world is thy command;
Vast as eternity, thy love:
Firm as a rock thy truth must stand
When rolling years shall cease to move.

8. Descend from heaven, immortal Dove!
Stoop down, and take us on thy wings;
And mount, and bear us far above
The reach of these inferior things.

Oh for a sight, a blissful sight,
Of our Almighty Father's throne!
There sits our Saviour crowned with light,
Clothed in a body like our own.

Adoring saints around him stand,
And thrones and powers before him fall:
The God shines gracious through the man,
And sheds sweet glories on them all.

When shall the day, dear Lord, appear,
That I shall mount to dwell above,
And stand and bow among them there,
And view thy face, and sing and love?

Songs for Home-Worship.

SEASONS. L. M.

9. Happy the man whose hopes rely
On Israel's God: he made the sky,
And earth and seas, with all their train;
And none shall find his promise vain.

His truth forever stands secure:
He saves the oppressed; he feeds the poor;
He sends the laboring conscience peace;
And grants the prisoner sweet release.

The Lord hath eyes to give the blind;
The Lord supports the sinking mind:
He helps the stranger in distress,
The widow, and the fatherless.

He loves his saints; he knows them well;
But turns the wicked down to hell.
Thy God, O Zion! ever reigns:
Praise him in everlasting strains.

10. Might I enjoy the meanest place,
Within thy house, O God of grace!
Not tents of ease, nor thrones of power,
Should tempt my feet to leave the door.

God is our sun; he makes our day:
God is our shield; he guards our way
From all the assaults of hell and sin,
From foes without and foes within.

All needful grace will God bestow,
And crown that grace with glory too:
He gives us all things, and withholds
No real good from upright souls.

O God our King, whose sovereign sway
The glorious hosts of heaven obey!
Display thy grace, exert thy power,
Till all on earth thy name adore.

DOWNS. C. M.

11. Father of mercies, in thy word
What endless glory shines!
Forever be thy name adored
For these celestial lines.

Here my Redeemer's welcome voice
Spreads heavenly peace around;
And life and everlasting joys
Attend the blissful sound.

Oh, may these heavenly pages be
My ever-dear delight!
And still new beauties may I see,
And still-increasing light!

Divine Instructor, gracious Lord,
Be thou forever near;
Teach me to love thy sacred Word,
And view my Saviour there.

12. Why should the children of a King
Go mourning all their days?
Great Comforter! descend, and bring
Some tokens of thy grace.

Dost thou not dwell in all the saints,
And seal them heirs of heaven?
When wilt thou banish my complaints,
And show my sins forgiven?

Assure my conscience of her part
In the Redeemer's blood;
And bear thy witness with my heart
That I am born of God.

Thou art the earnest of his love,
The pledge of joys to come;
And thy soft wings, celestial Dove,
Will safe convey me home.

Songs for Home-Worship.

TRURO. L. M.

Spirited. — Dr. Burney.

13.
Another six-days' work is done;
Another Sabbath is begun:
Return, my soul, unto thy rest;
Enjoy the day thy God hath blest.

Oh that our thoughts and thanks may rise
As grateful incense to the skies,
And draw from heaven that sweet repose
Which none but he that feels it knows!

That heavenly calm within the breast —
It is the pledge of that dear rest
Which for the Church of God remains, —
The end of cares, the end of pains.

In holy duties let the day,
In holy pleasures, pass away:
How sweet a Sabbath thus to spend
In hope of one that ne'er shall end!

14.
O God! beneath thy guiding hand
Our exiled fathers crossed the sea;
And, when they trod the wintry strand,
With prayer and psalm they worshipped thee.

Thou heard'st, well pleased, the song, the prayer:
Thy blessing came; and still its power
Shall onward through all ages bear
The memory of that holy hour.

Laws, freedom, truth, and faith in God,
Came with those exiles o'er the waves;
And, where their pilgrim-feet have trod,
The God they trusted guards their graves.

And here thy name, O God of love,
Their children's children shall adore,
Till these eternal hills remove,
And spring adorns the earth no more.

STEPHENS. C. M.

Spirited.

15.
Come, Holy Spirit, Heavenly Dove,
With all thy quickening powers;
Kindle a flame of sacred love
In these cold hearts of ours.

Look, how we grovel here below,
Fond of these trifling toys!
Our souls can neither fly nor go
To reach eternal joys.

Dear Lord, and shall we ever live
At this poor dying rate?
Our love so faint, so cold to thee,
And thine to us so great!

Come, Holy Spirit, Heavenly Dove,
With all thy quickening powers;
Come, shed abroad a Saviour's love,
And that shall kindle ours.

16.
Come, let us join our cheerful songs
With angels round the throne:
Ten thousand thousand are their tongues;
But all their joys are one.

"Worthy the Lamb that died," they cry,
"To be exalted thus:"
"Worthy the Lamb," our lips reply;
"For he was slain for us."

Jesus is worthy to receive
Honor and power divine:
And blessings more than we can give
Be, Lord, forever thine.

Let all that dwell above the sky,
And air and earth and seas,
Conspire to lift thy glories high,
And speak thine endless praise.

Songs for Home-Worship.

ROCKINGHAM. L. M.   Dr. Lowell Mason.

17. How pleasant, how divinely fair,
O Lord of hosts! thy dwellings are!
With long desire my spirit faints
To meet the assemblies of thy saints.

Blest are the souls who find a place
Within the temple of thy grace:
There they behold thy gentler rays,
And seek thy face, and learn thy praise.

Blest are the men whose hearts are set
To find the way to Zion's gate:
God is their strength; and through the road
They lean upon their helper, God.

Cheerful they walk with growing strength
Till all shall meet in heaven at length;
Till all before thy face appear,
And join in nobler worship there.

18. The heavens declare thy glory, Lord;
In every star thy wisdom shines:
But, when our eyes behold thy Word,
We read thy name in fairer lines.

The rolling sun, the changing light,
And nights and days, thy power confess;
But the blest volume thou hast writ
Reveals thy justice and thy grace.

Sun, moon, and stars convey thy praise
Round the whole earth, and never stand:
So, when thy truth began its race,
It touched and glanced on every land.

Great Sun of Righteousness, arise!
Bless the dark world with heavenly light:
Thy gospel makes the simple wise;
Thy laws are pure, thy judgments right.

FULLER. C. M.

19. On Jordan's stormy banks I stand,
And cast a wishful eye
To Canaan's fair and happy land,
Where my possessions lie.

O'er all those wide-extended plains
Shines one eternal day:
There God the Son forever reigns,
And scatters night away.

When shall I reach that happy place,
And be forever blest?
When shall I see my Father's face,
And in his bosom rest?

Filled with delight, my raptured soul
Can here no longer stay:
Though Jordan's waves around me roll,
Fearless I'd launch away.

20. Far from these narrow scenes of night
Unbounded glories rise,
And realms of infinite delight
Unknown to mortal eyes.

There pain and sickness never come,
And grief no more complains:
Health triumphs in immortal bloom,
And endless pleasure reigns.

No cloud those blissful regions know,
Forever bright and fair;
For sin, the source of mortal woe,
Can never enter there.

Prepare us, Lord, by grace divine,
For thy bright courts on high;
Then bid our spirits rise, and join
The chorus of the sky.

Songs for Home-Worship.

UXBRIDGE. L. M.

21.
O Lord! thy heavenly grace impart,
And fix my frail, inconstant heart:
Henceforth my chief desire shall be
To dedicate myself to thee.

Whate'er pursuits my time employ,
One thought shall fill my soul with joy:
That silent, secret thought shall be,
That all my hopes are fixed on thee.

Thy glorious eye pervadeth space;
Thy presence, Lord, fills every place;
And, wheresoe'er my lot may be,
Still shall my spirit cleave to thee.

Renouncing every worldly thing,
And safe beneath thy spreading wing,
My sweetest thought henceforth shall be,
That all I want I find in thee.

22.
Thee we adore, Eternal Lord;
We praise thy name with one accord:
Thy saints, who here thy goodness see,
Through all the world do worship thee.

To thee aloud all angels cry,
The heavens, and all the powers on high:
Thee, holy, holy, holy King,
Lord God of hosts, they ever sing.

The apostles join the glorious throng;
The prophets swell the immortal song;
The martyrs' noble army raise
Eternal anthems to thy praise.

From day to day, O Lord! do we
Highly exalt and honor thee:
Thy name we worship and adore,
World without end, for evermore.

MANOAH. C. M.

23.
See! Jesus stands with open arms;
He calls; he bids you come:
Guilt holds you back, and fear alarms;
But, see! there yet is room.

Oh! come, and with his children taste
The blessings of his love,
While hope attends the sweet repast
Of nobler joys above.

There with united heart and voice,
Before the eternal throne,
Ten thousand thousand souls rejoice
In ecstasies unknown.

And yet ten thousand thousand more
Are welcome still to come:
Ye longing souls, the grace adore;
Approach; there yet is room.

24.
There is a fold whence none can stray,
And pastures ever green,
Where sultry sun, or stormy day,
Or night, is never seen.

Far up the everlasting hills,
In God's own light, it lies;
His smile its vast dimensions fills
With joy that never dies.

One narrow vale, one darksome wave,
Divides that land from this:
I have a Shepherd pledged to save,
And bear me home to bliss.

O gentle Shepherd! still behold
Thy helpless charge in me,
And take a wanderer to thy fold
Who trembling turns to thee.

Songs for Home-Worship.

WARD. L. M.
Dr. L. Mason.

25. Faith to the conscience whispers peace,
And bids the mourner's sighing cease:
By faith the children's right we claim,
And call upon our Father's name.

Faith feels the Spirit's kindling breath
In love and hope that conquer death;
Faith brings us to delight in God,
And blesses e'en his smiting rod.

Such faith in us, O God! implant,
And to our prayers thy favor grant
In Jesus Christ, thy saving Son,
Who is our fount of health alone.

In him may every trusting soul
Press onward to the heavenly goal,
The blessedness no foes destroy, —
Eternal love and light and joy!

26. With tearful eyes I look around;
Life seems a dark and stormy sea;
Yet 'midst the gloom I hear a sound,
A heavenly whisper, "Come to Me!"

It tells me of a place of rest;
It tells me where my soul may flee:
Oh! to the weary, faint, opprest,
How sweet the bidding, "Come to Me!"

"Come; for all else must fail and die:
Earth is no resting-place for thee.
To heaven direct thy weeping eye:
I am thy portion; come to Me!"

O voice of mercy, voice of love!
In conflict, grief, and agony,
Support me, cheer me from above,
And gently whisper, "Come to Me!"

WARWICK. C. M.

27. My God, thy service well demands
The remnant of my days:
Why was this fleeting breath renewed,
But to renew thy praise?

Thine arm of everlasting love
Did this weak frame sustain
When life was hovering o'er the grave,
And nature sank with pain.

Back from the borders of the grave,
At thy command, I come;
Nor would I urge a speedier flight
To my celestial home.

Where thou appointest my abode,
There would I choose to be;
For in thy presence death is life,
And earth is heaven with thee.

28. Oh for a closer walk with God,
A calm and heavenly frame,
A light to shine upon the road
That leads me to the Lamb!

Return, O Holy Dove! return,
Sweet messenger of rest!
I hate the sins that made thee mourn,
And drove thee from my breast.

The dearest idol I have known,
Whate'er that idol be,
Help me to tear it from thy throne,
And worship only thee.

So shall my walk be close with God,
Calm and serene my frame;
So purer light shall mark the road
That leads me to the Lamb.

Songs for Home-Worship.

FEDERAL STREET. L. M.   H. K. OLIVER.

29. Praise, Lord, for thee in Zion waits;
Prayer shall besiege thy temple-gates:
All flesh shall to thy throne repair,
And find, through Christ, salvation there.

How blest thy saints! how safely led!
How surely kept! how richly fed!
Saviour of all in earth and sea,
How happy they who rest in thee!

Thy hand sets fast the mighty hills;
Thy voice the troubled ocean stills:
Evening and morning hymn thy praise,
And earth thy bounty wide displays.

The year is with thy goodness crowned;
Thy clouds drop wealth the world around;
Through thee the deserts laugh and sing;
And Nature smiles, and owns her King.

30. When I survey the wondrous cross
On which the Prince of glory died,
My richest gain I count but loss,
And pour contempt on all my pride.

Forbid it, Lord, that I should boast,
Save in the death of Christ my God:
All the vain things that charm me most,
I sacrifice them to his blood.

See! from his head, his hands, his feet,
Sorrow and love flow mingled down!
Did e'er such love and sorrow meet,
Or thorns compose so rich a crown?

Were the whole realm of Nature mine,
That were a present far too small:
Love so amazing, so divine,
Demands my soul, my life, my all.

WARRINGTON. L. M.

31. The spacious firmament on high,
With all the blue, ethereal sky,
And spangled heavens, a shining frame,
Their great Original proclaim.

The unwearied sun, from day to day,
Does his Creator's power display,
And publishes to every land
The work of an almighty hand.

Soon as the evening shades prevail,
The moon takes up the wondrous tale,
And nightly to the listening earth
Repeats the story of her birth;

While all the stars that round her burn,
And all the planets in their turn,
Confirm the tidings as they roll,
And spread the truth from pole to pole.

32. God of my life! through all my days
My grateful powers shall sound thy praise;
The song shall wake with opening light,
And warble to the silent night.

When anxious care would break my rest,
And grief would tear my throbbing breast,
Thy tuneful praises raised on high
Shall check the murmur and the sigh.

When Death o'er Nature shall prevail,
And all my powers of language fail,
Joy through my swimming eyes shall break,
And mean the thanks I cannot speak.

Soon shall I learn the exalted strains
Which echo o'er the heavenly plains,
And emulate with joy unknown
The glowing seraphs round thy throne.

Songs for Home-Worship.

HEBRON. L. M.
Dr. Lowell Mason.

33. Thus far, the Lord hath led me on;
　Thus far, his power prolongs my days;
And every evening shall make known
　Some fresh memorials of his grace.

I lay my body down to sleep:
　Peace is the pillow for my head;
While well-appointed angels keep
　Their watchful stations round my bed.

Faith in His name forbids my fear:
　Oh, may Thy presence ne'er depart!
And, in the morning, make me hear
　The love and kindness of thy heart.

Thus, when the night of death shall come,
　My flesh shall rest beneath the ground,
And wait thy voice to rouse my tomb,
　With sweet salvation in the sound.

34. Why should we start, and fear to die?
　What timorous worms we mortals are!
Death is the gate of endless joy;
　And yet we dread to enter there.

The pains, the groans, and dying strife,
　Fright our approaching souls away;
Still we shrink back again to life,
　Fond of our prison and our clay.

Oh! if my Lord would come and meet,
　My soul should stretch her wings in haste,
Fly fearless through Death's iron gate,
　Nor feel the terrors as she passed.

Jesus can make a dying-bed
　Feel soft as downy pillows are,
While on his breast I lean my head,
　And breathe my life out sweetly there.

ST. GABRIEL. L. M.

35. Sun of my soul, thou Saviour dear,
　It is not night if thou be near;
Oh, may no earth-born cloud arise
　To hide thee from thy servant's eyes!

Abide with me from morn till eve;
　For without thee I cannot live;
Abide with me when night is nigh;
　For without thee I dare not die.

Thou Framer of the light and dark,
　Guide through the tempest thine own bark;
Amid the howling, wintry sea,
　We are in port, if we have thee.

Come near and bless us when we wake,
　Ere through the world our way we take,
Till in the ocean of thy love
　We lose ourselves in heaven above.

36. God, in the gospel of his Son,
　Makes his eternal counsels known;
'Tis here his richest mercy shines,
　And truth is drawn in fairest lines.

Here sinners of a humble frame
　May taste his grace, and learn his name;
May read in characters of blood
　The wisdom, power, and grace of God.

The prisoner here may break his chains,
　The weary rest from all his pains,
The captive feel his bondage cease,
　The mourner find the way of peace.

Here faith reveals to mortal eyes
　A brighter world beyond the skies;
Here shines the light which guides our way
　From earth to realms of endless day.

Songs for Home-Worship.

EVENING HYMN. L. M.
Tallis.

37.
Glory to thee, my God, this night,
For all the blessings of the light:
Keep me, oh! keep me, King of kings,
Beneath thine own almighty wings.

Forgive me, Lord, for thy dear Son,
The ill that I this day have done;
That with the world, myself, and thee,
I, ere I sleep, at peace may be.

Be thou my guardian while I sleep;
Thy watchful station near me keep;
My heart with love celestial fill,
And guard me from the approach of ill.

Praise God, from whom all blessings flow;
Praise him, all creatures here below;
Praise him above, ye heavenly host, —
Praise Father, Son, and Holy Ghost.

38.
Come, O my soul! in sacred lays
Attempt thy great Creator's praise:
But, oh! what tongue can speak his fame?
What mortal verse can reach the theme?

Enthroned amid the radiant spheres,
He glory, like a garment, wears:
To form a robe of light divine,
Ten thousand suns around him shine.

In all our Maker's grand designs,
Almighty power with wisdom shines:
His works, through all this wondrous frame,
Declare the glory of his name.

Raised on Devotion's lofty wing,
Do thou, my soul, his glories sing;
And let his praise employ thy tongue
Till listening worlds shall join the song.

ST. THOMAS. S. M.
A. Williams.

39.
My soul, it is thy God
Who calls thee by his grace:
Now loose thee from each cumbering load,
And bend thee to the race.

Make thy salvation sure;
All sloth and slumber shun;
Nor dare a moment rest secure
Till thou the goal hast won.

Thy crown of life hold fast;
Thy heart with courage stay;
Nor let one trembling glance be cast
Along the backward way.

Thy path ascends the skies
With conquering footsteps bright;
And thou shalt win and wear the prize
In everlasting light.

40.
How perfect is thy word,
And all thy judgments just!
Forever sure thy promise, Lord,
And men securely trust.

I hear thy word with love,
And I would fain obey:
Send thy good Spirit from above
To guide me, lest I stray.

Warn me of every sin;
Forgive my secret faults:
And cleanse this guilty soul of mine,
Whose crimes exceed my thoughts.

While with my heart and tongue
I spread thy praise abroad,
Accept the worship and the song,
My Saviour and my God.

Songs for Home-Worship.

Words by BONAR.   **NEVERMORE BE SAD OR WEARY. 8s and 7s.**   THEO. F. SEWARD.

41.
This is not my place of resting;
Mine's a city yet to come:
Onward to it I am hasting,—
On to my eternal home.

In it all is light and glory;
O'er it shines a nightless day:
Every trace of sin's sad story,
All the curse, hath passed away.

There the Lamb, our Shepherd, leads us
By the streams of life along;
On the freshest pastures feeds us;
Turns our sighing into song.

Soon we pass this desert dreary;
Soon we bid farewell to pain;
Never more are sad or weary;
Never, never sin again.

42.
Cease, ye mourners! cease to languish
O'er the grave of those you love:
Pain and death, and night and anguish,
Enter not the world above.

While our silent steps are straying
Lonely through night's deepening shade,
Glory's brightest beams are playing
Round the happy Christian's head.

Light and peace at once deriving
From the hand of God most high,
In his glorious presence living,
They shall never, never die.

Now, ye mourners! cease to languish
O'er the grave of those you love:
Far removed from pain and anguish,
They are chanting hymns above.

SEYMOUR. 7s.

43.
To thy pastures fair and large,
Heavenly Shepherd, lead thy charge;
And my couch, with tenderest care,
'Mid the springing grass prepare.

When I faint with summer's heat,
Thou shalt guide my weary feet
To the streams, that, still and slow,
Through the verdant meadows flow.

Safe the dreary vale I tread,
By the shades of death o'erspread,
With thy rod and staff supplied,—
This my guard, and that my guide.

Constant to my latest end
Thou my footsteps shalt attend,
And shalt bid thy hallowed dome
Yield me an eternal home.

44.
Now the shades of night are gone;
Now the morning light is come.
Lord, we would be thine to-day:
Drive the shades of sin away.

Fill our souls with heavenly light;
Banish doubt, and clear our sight:
In thy service, Lord, to-day,
Help us labor, help us pray.

Keep our wayward passions bound;
Save us from our foes around;
Going out and coming in,
Keep us safe from every sin.

When our work of life is past,
Oh! receive us all at last:
Sin's dark night shall be no more
When we reach the heavenly shore.

Songs for Home-Worship.

Adagio e Piano.   LUCERNE. L. M.

45. How vain is all beneath the skies!
How transient every earthly bliss!
How slender all the fondest ties
That bind us to a world like this?

The evening cloud, the morning dew,
The withering grass, the fading flower,
Of earthly hopes are emblems true,
The glory of a passing hour.

But though Earth's fairest blossoms die,
And all beneath the skies is vain,
There is a land whose confines lie
Beyond the reach of care and pain.

Then let the hope of joys to come
Dispel our cares, and chase our fears:
If God be ours, we're travelling home,
Though passing through a vale of tears.

46. How blest the righteous when he dies!
When sinks a weary soul to rest.
How mildly beam the closing eyes!
How gently heaves the expiring breast!

So fades a summer cloud away;
So sinks the gale when storms are o'er;
So gently shuts the eye of day;
So dies the wave along the shore.

A holy quiet reigns around,
A calm which life nor death destroys:
Nothing disturbs that peace profound
Which his unfettered soul enjoys.

Life's duty done, as sinks the clay,
Light from its load the spirit flies;
While heaven and earth combine to say,
"How blest the righteous when he dies!"

Moderato.   OLNEY. S. M.

47. When we in darkness walk,
Nor feel the heavenly flame,
Then is the time to trust our God,
And rest upon his name.

Soon shall our doubts and fears
Subside at his control;
His loving-kindness shall break through
The midnight of the soul.

His grace will to the end
Stronger and brighter shine;
Nor present things, nor things to come,
Shall quench the spark divine.

Blest is the man, O God!
That stays himself on thee:
Who waits for thy salvation, Lord,
Shall thy salvation see.

48. My spirit on thy care,
Blest Saviour, I recline:
Thou wilt not leave me to despair;
For thou art love divine.

In thee I place my trust;
On thee I calmly rest;
I know thee good, I know thee just,
And count thy choice the best.

Whate'er events betide,
Thy will they all perform:
Safe in thy breast my head I hide,
Nor fear the coming storm.

Let good or ill befall,
It must be good for me,
Secure of having thee in all,
Of having all in thee.

Songs for Home-Worship.

PARK STREET. L. M.
Con Spirito. VENUA.

49. Jesus shall reign where'er the sun
Doth his successive journeys run;
His kingdom stretch from shore to shore
Till moons shall wax and wane no more.

For him shall endless prayer be made,
And praises throng to crown his head;
His name, like sweet perfume, shall rise
With every morning sacrifice.

Blessings abound where'er he reigns:
The prisoner leaps to loose his chains,
The weary find eternal rest,
And all the sons of Want are blest.

Let every creature rise, and bring
Peculiar honors to our King;
Angels descend with songs again,
And earth repeat the loud Amen.

50. Sweet is the work, my God, my King,
To praise thy name, give thanks, and sing;
To show thy love by morning light,
And talk of all thy truth at night.

My heart shall triumph in my Lord,
And bless his works, and bless his word:
Thy works of grace — how bright they shine!
How deep thy counsels! how divine!

But I shall share a glorious part
When grace hath well refined my heart,
And fresh supplies of joy are shed,
Like holy oil, to cheer my head.

Then shall I see and hear and know
All I desired or wished below,
And every power find sweet employ
In that eternal world of joy.

MORNINGTON. S. M.
LORD MORNINGTON.

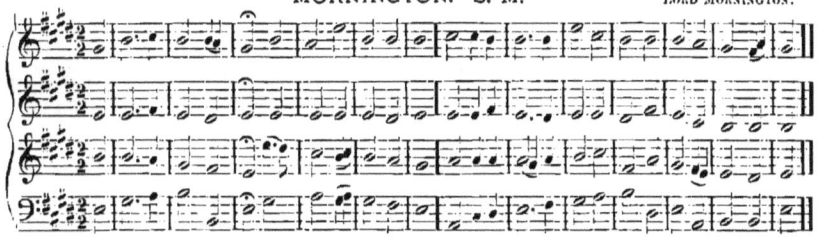

51. One sweetly-solemn thought
Comes to me o'er and o'er:
'Tis that I'm nearer home to day
Than e'er I've been before;

Nearer my Father's house,
Where many mansions be;
Nearer the solemn judgment-throne;
Nearer the crystal sea;

Nearer the bound where life
Shall lay its burdens down;
Where I shall leave my ill-borne cross,
And take my blood-bought crown.

Saviour, perfect my trust;
Confirm my feeble faith;
And teach me fearlessly to stand
Upon the shore of death.

52. How charming is the place
Where my Redeemer, God,
Unveils the beauties of his face,
And sheds his love abroad!

Here on the mercy-seat,
With radiant glories crowned,
Our joyful eyes behold him sit,
And smile on all around.

To him our prayers and cries
Our humble souls present;
He listens to our broken sighs,
And grants us every want.

Give me, O Lord! a place
Within thy blest abode,
Among the children of thy grace,
The servants of my God.

Songs for Home-Worship.

DOVER. S. M.

53. Blest are the sons of peace
Whose hearts and hopes are one;
Whose kind designs to serve and please
Through all their actions run.

Blest is the pious house
Where zeal and friendship meet:
Their songs of praise, their mingled vows,
Make their communion sweet.

From those celestial springs
Such streams of pleasure flow,
As no increase of riches brings,
Nor honors can bestow.

Thus on the heavenly hills
The saints are blest above,
Where joy, like morning dew, distils,
And all the air is love.

54. My soul, repeat His praise
Whose mercies are so great;
Whose anger is so slow to rise,
So ready to abate.

God will not always chide:
And, when his wrath is felt,
Its strokes are fewer than our crimes,
And lighter than our guilt.

His power subdues our sins;
And his forgiving love,
Far as the east is from the west,
Doth all our guilt remove.

High as the heavens are raised
Above the ground we tread,
So far the riches of his grace
Our highest thoughts exceed.

CARROLL. L. M. — Dr. L. Mason.

55. Great God, we sing thy mighty hand,
By which supported still we stand:
The opening year thy mercy shows;
Let mercy crown it till it close.

By day, by night, at home, abroad,
Still we are guarded by our God,
By his incessant bounty fed,
By his unerring counsel led.

With grateful hearts the past we own:
The future, all to us unknown,
We to thy guardian care commit,
And peaceful leave before thy feet.

When Death shall interrupt these songs,
And seal in silence mortal tongues,
Our helper, God, in whom we trust,
In better worlds our souls shall boast.

56. Up to the hills I lift mine eyes,—
The eternal hills beyond the skies;
Thence all her help my soul derives,
There my almighty Refuge lives.

He lives!—the everlasting God
That built the world, that spread the flood:
The heavens with all their hosts he made,
And the dark regions of the dead.

He guides our feet, he guards our way;
His morning smiles bless all the day;
He spreads the evening veil, and keeps
The silent hours while Israel sleeps.

Praise God, from whom all blessings flow;
Praise him, all creatures here below;
Praise him above, ye heavenly host,—
Praise Father, Son, and Holy Ghost.

Songs for Home-Worship.

CHESTERFIELD. C. M.

57. Oh for a faith that will not shrink,
   Though pressed by every foe;
   That will not tremble on the brink
   Of any earthly woe;

A faith that shines more bright and clear
   When tempests rage without;
That when in danger knows no fear,
   In darkness feels no doubt;

That bears, unmoved, the world's dread frown,
   Nor heeds its scornful smile;
That seas of trouble cannot drown,
   Nor Satan's arts beguile;

A faith that keeps the narrow way
   Till life's last hour is fled,
And with a pure and heavenly ray
   Lights up a dying-bed!

58. When God revealed his gracious name,
   And changed my mournful state,
My rapture seemed a pleasing dream,
   The grace appeared so great.

The world beheld the glorious change,
   And did Thy hand confess;
My tongue broke out in unknown strains,
   And sung surprising grace.

The Lord can clear the darkest skies;
   Can give us day for night;
Make drops of sacred sorrow rise
   To rivers of delight.

Let those who sow in sadness wait
   Till the fair harvest come:
They shall confess their sheaves are great,
   And shout the blessings home.

ST. MICHAEL. C. M.

59. What shall I render to my God
   For all his kindness shown?
My feet shall visit thine abode,
   My songs address thy throne.

How much is mercy thy delight,
   Thou ever-blessed God!
How dear thy servants in thy sight!
   How precious is their blood!

How happy all thy servants are!
   How great thy grace to me!
My life, which thou hast made thy care,
   Lord, I devote to thee.

Now I am thine, forever thine;
   Nor shall my purpose move:
Thy hand hath loosed my bonds of pain,
   And bound me with thy love.

60. Faith adds new charms to earthly bliss,
   And saves me from its snares;
Its aid in every duty brings,
   And softens all my cares.

Wide it unveils celestial worlds,
   Where deathless pleasures reign;
And bids me seek my portion there,
   Nor bids me seek in vain.

Faith shows the precious promise sealed
   With the Redeemer's blood,
And helps my feeble hope to rest
   Upon a faithful God.

There, there, unshaken would I rest
   Till this frail body dies;
And then, on Faith's triumphant wings,
   To endless glory rise.

Songs for Home-Worship.

PETERBOROUGH. C. M.

61. Come, Lord, and warm each languid heart;
Inspire each lifeless tongue;
And let the joys of heaven impart
Their influence to our song.

Then to the shining realms of bliss
The wings of faith shall soar,
And all the charms of Paradise
Our raptured thoughts explore.

Sorrow and pain and tears and care
And discord there shall cease,
And perfect joy and love sincere
Adorn the realms of peace.

Lord, tune our hearts to praise and love;
Our feeble notes inspire;
Till in thy blissful courts above
We join the heavenly choir.

62. Happy the souls to Jesus joined,
And saved by grace alone:
Walking in all Thy ways, they find
Their heaven on earth begun.

The Church triumphant in thy love,
Their mighty joys we know:
They sing the Lamb in hymns above,
And we in hymns below.

Thee in thy glorious realm they praise,
And bow before thy throne;
We in the kingdom of thy grace:
The kingdoms are but one.

The holy to the Holiest leads;
From hence our spirits rise:
And he that in thy statutes treads
Shall meet thee in the skies.

ORTONVILLE. C. M. — Dr. T. Hastings.

63. How sweet, how heavenly, is the sight,
When those that love the Lord
In one another's peace delight,
And so fulfil his word;

When each can feel his brother's sigh,
And with him bear a part;
When sorrow flows from eye to eye,
And joy from heart to heart;

When, free from envy, scorn, and pride,
Our wishes all above,
Each can his brother's failings hide,
And show a brother's love!

Love is the golden chain that binds
The happy souls above;
And he's an heir of heaven who finds
His bosom glow with love.

64. Awake, my soul! stretch every nerve,
And press with vigor on:
A heavenly race demands thy zeal,
And an immortal crown.

'Tis God's all-animating voice
That calls thee from on high;
'Tis his own hand presents the prize
To thine aspiring eye,—

That prize with peerless glories bright,
Which shall new lustre boast
When victors' wreaths and monarchs' gems
Shall blend in common dust.

Blest Saviour, introduced by thee,
Have I my race begun;
And, crowned with victory, at thy feet
I'll lay my honors down.

Songs for Home-Worship.

COLCHESTER. C. M. — WILLIAMS.

65.
How shall the young secure their hearts,
And guard their lives from sin?
Thy Word the choicest rule imparts,
To keep the conscience clean.

'Tis like the sun, a heavenly light,
That guides us all the day;
And, through the dangers of the night,
A lamp to lead our way.

Thy precepts make me truly wise:
I hate the sinner's road;
I hate my own vain thoughts that rise;
But love thy law, my God.

Thy word is everlasting truth:
How pure is every page!
That holy book shall guide our youth,
And well support our age.

66.
When the worn spirit wants repose,
And sighs her God to seek,
How sweet to hail the evening's close
That ends the weary week!

How sweet to hail the early dawn
That opens on the sight
When first that soul-reviving morn
Beams its new rays of light!

Sweet day! thine hours too soon will cease;
Yet, while they gently roll,
Breathe, heavenly Spirit, Source of peace,
A sabbath o'er my soul.

When will my pilgrimage be done,
The world's long week be o'er,
That sabbath dawn which needs no sun,
That day which fades no more?

NEWHOPE. C. M.

67.
Oh for a heart to praise my God;
A heart from sin set free;
A heart that's sprinkled with the blood
So freely shed for me;

An humble, lowly, contrite heart,
Believing, true, and clean,
Which neither life nor death can part
From Him that dwells within;

A heart in every thought renewed,
And filled with love divine;
Perfect and right and pure and good;
A copy, Lord, of thine!

Thy nature, dearest Lord, impart;
Come quickly from above;
Write thy new name upon my heart,—
Thy new, best name of Love.

68.
Whilst thee I seek, protecting Power,
Be my vain wishes stilled;
And may this consecrated hour
With better hopes be filled!

Thy love the power of thought bestowed;
To thee my thoughts would soar:
Thy mercy o'er my life has flowed;
That mercy I adore.

In each event of life, how clear
Thy ruling hand I see!
Each blessing to my soul more dear
Because conferred by thee.

In every joy that crowns my days,
In every pain I bear,
My heart shall find delight in praise,
Or seek relief in prayer.

Songs for Home-Worship.

MONTGOMERY. L. M.
T. B. Mason.

69. Jehovah reigns!—he dwells in light,
Girded with majesty and might:
The world, created by his hands,
Still on its firm foundation stands.

But ere this spacious world was made,
Or had its first foundation laid,
Thy throne eternal ages stood,
Thyself the ever-living God.

Like floods the angry nations rise,
And aim their rage against the skies:
Vain floods, that aim their rage so high!
At thy rebuke the billows die.

Forever shall thy throne endure;
Thy promise stand forever sure;
And everlasting holiness
Becomes the dwelling of thy grace.

70. All people that on earth do dwell,
Sing to the Lord with cheerful voice;
Him serve with fear, his praise forth tell;
Come ye before him, and rejoice.

The Lord, ye know, is God indeed;
Without our aid he did us make:
We are his flock; he doth us feed;
And for his sheep he doth us take.

Oh! enter, then, his gates with praise;
Approach with joy his courts unto:
Praise, laud, and bless his name always;
For it is seemly so to do.

For why? the Lord our God is good;
His mercy is for ever sure:
His truth at all times firmly stood,
And shall from age to age endure.

WINCHESTER. L. M.
Dr. Croft.

71. Asleep in Jesus!—blessed sleep!
From which none ever wake to weep;
A calm and undisturbed repose,
Unbroken by the last of foes.

Asleep in Jesus!—oh, how sweet
To be for such a slumber meet;
With holy confidence to sing
That death hath lost its venomed sting!

Asleep in Jesus!—peaceful rest,
Whose waking is supremely blest:
No fear, no woe, shall dim that hour
Which manifests the Saviour's power.

Asleep in Jesus!—oh, for me
May such a blissful refuge be!
Securely shall my ashes lie,
And wait the summons from on high.

72. "We've no abiding city here;"
Sad truth, were this to be our home;
But let this thought our spirits cheer,
"We seek a city yet to come."

"We've no abiding city here;"
We seek a city out of sight,
Zion its name: the Lord is there;
It shines with everlasting light.

O sweet abode of peace and love,
Where pilgrims freed from toil are blest!
Had I the pinions of the dove,
I'd fly to thee, and be at rest.

But hush, my soul! nor dare repine;
The time my God appoints is best;
While here, to do his will be mine,
And his to fix my time of rest.

Songs for Home-Worship.

LEAMING. L. M.
Italian Melody.

73.
No more, my God, I boast no more,
Of all the duties I have done:
I quit the hopes I held before
To trust the merits of thy Son.

Now for the love I bear his name,
What was my gain I count my loss:
My former pride I call my shame,
And nail my glory to his cross.

Yes, and I must and will esteem
All things but loss for Jesus' sake:
Oh, may my soul be found in him,
And of his righteousness partake!

The best obedience of my hands
Dares not appear before thy throne;
But faith can answer thy demands
By pleading what my Lord has done.

74.
Jesus, my all, to heaven is gone,—
He whom I fix my hopes upon:
His track I see, and I'll pursue
The narrow way till him I view.

This is the way I long have sought,
And mourned because I found it not;
Till late I heard my Saviour say,
"Come hither, soul; I am the way."

Lo! glad I come; and thou, blest Lamb!
Wilt take me to thee as I am:
Nothing but sin I thee can give;
Nothing but love shall I receive.

Now will I tell to sinners round
How dear a Saviour I have found:
I'll point to thy redeeming blood,
And say, "Behold the way to God!"

AZMON. C. M.
Glaser.

75.
Majestic sweetness sits enthroned
Upon the Saviour's brow;
His head with radiant glories crowned,
His lips with grace o'erflow.

No mortal can with him compare
Among the sons of men:
Fairer is he than all the fair
That fill the heavenly train.

To him I owe my life and breath,
And all the joys I have:
He makes me triumph over death;
He saves me from the grave.

Since from his bounty I receive
Such proofs of love divine,
Had I a thousand hearts to give,
Lord, they should all be thine.

76.
Thou art the Way: to thee alone
From sin and death we flee;
And he who would the Father seek,
Must seek him, Lord, by thee.

Thou art the Truth: thy word alone
True wisdom can impart:
Thou only canst inform the mind,
And purify the heart.

Thou art the Life: the rending tomb
Proclaims thy conquering arm;
And those who put their trust in thee
Nor death nor hell shall harm.

Thou art the Way, the Truth, the Life:
Grant us that way to know,
That truth to keep, that life to win,
Whose joys eternal flow.

Songs for Home-Worship.

DENNIS. S. M. *Arranged from* NAGELI.

77.
If through unruffled seas
Toward heaven we calmly sail,
With grateful hearts, O God! to thee
We'll own the fostering gale.

But should the surges rise,
And rest delay to come,
Blest be the sorrow, kind the storm,
Which drives us nearer home.

Soon shall our doubts and fears
All yield to thy control:
Thy tender mercies shall illume
The midnight of the soul.

Teach us, in every state,
To make thy will our own;
And, when the joys of sense depart,
To live by faith alone.

78.
Blest are the pure in heart;
For they shall see their God:
The secret of the Lord is theirs;
Their soul is Christ's abode.

The Lord, who left the heavens
Our life and peace to bring,
To dwell in lowliness with men,
Their Pattern and their King, —

He to the lowly soul
Doth still himself impart,
And for his dwelling and his throne
Chooseth the pure in heart.

Lord, we thy presence seek:
May ours this blessing be!
Oh! give the pure and lowly heart
A temple meet for thee.

ARMENIA. C. M. S. B. POND.

79.
With joy we hail the sacred day
Which God hath called his own;
With joy the summons we obey
To worship at his throne.

Thy chosen temple, Lord, how fair!
Where willing votaries throng
To breathe the humble, fervent prayer,
And pour the choral song.

Let peace within her walls be found;
Let all her sons unite
To spread with grateful zeal around
Her clear and shining light.

Great God! we hail the sacred day
Which thou hast called thine own;
With joy the summons we obey
To worship at thy throne.

80.
Lift up your heads, eternal gates!
Unfold to entertain
The King of glory: see! he comes
With his celestial train.

Who is this King of glory? who?
The Lord, for strength renowned,
In battle mighty; o'er his foes
Eternal victor crowned.

Lift up your heads, ye gates! unfold
In state to entertain
The King of glory: see! he comes
With all his shining train.

Who is this King of glory? who?
The Lord of hosts renowned:
Of glory he alone is King
Who is with glory crowned.

Songs for Home-Worship.

ZANESVILLE. C. M.

81.
God moves in a mysterious way
His wonders to perform:
He plants his footsteps in the sea,
And rides upon the storm.

Ye fearful saints, fresh courage take:
The clouds ye so much dread
Are big with mercy, and shall break
In blessings on your head.

His purposes will ripen fast,
Unfolding every hour:
The bud may have a bitter taste,
But sweet will be the flower.

Blind unbelief is sure to err,
And scan his work in vain:
God is his own interpreter,
And he will make it plain.

82.
Lord, in the morning thou shalt hear
My voice ascending high:
To thee will I direct my prayer,
To thee lift up mine eye.

Thou art a God before whose sight
The wicked shall not stand:
Sinners shall ne'er be thy delight,
Nor dwell at thy right hand.

But to thy house will I resort
To taste thy mercies there:
I will frequent thy holy court,
And worship in thy fear.

Oh, may thy Spirit guide my feet
In ways of righteousness;
Make every path of duty straight,
And plain before my face!

BADEA. S. M.

83.
Still with thee, O my God!
I would desire to be;
By day, by night, at home, abroad,
I would be still with thee:

With thee when dawn comes in,
And calls me back to care;
Each day returning to begin
With thee, my God, in prayer:

With thee when day is done,
And evening calms the mind;
The setting as the rising sun
With thee my heart would find:

With thee when darkness brings
The signal of repose;
Calm in the shadow of thy wings,
Mine eyelids I would close.

84.
Great is the Lord our God,
And let his praise be great:
He makes his churches his abode,
His most delightful seat.

These temples of his grace —
How beautiful they stand!
The honor of our native place,
And glory of our land.

Oft have our fathers told,
Our eyes have often seen,
How well our God secures the fold
Where his own sheep have been.

In every new distress
We'll to his house repair;
We'll think upon his wondrous grace,
And seek deliverance there.

Songs for Home-Worship.

DEVIZES. C. M.
TUCKER.

85. Let children hear the mighty deeds
Which God performed of old;
Which in our younger years we saw,
And which our fathers told.

He bids us make his glories known,
His works of power and grace;
And we'll convey his wonders down
Through every rising race.

Our lips shall tell them to our sons,
And they again to theirs,
That generations yet unborn
May teach them to their heirs.

Thus shall they learn in God alone
Their hope securely stands,
That they may ne'er forget his works,
But practise his commands.

86. With joy we meditate the grace
Of our High Priest above:
His heart is made of tenderness;
His bosom glows with love.

Touched with a sympathy within,
He knows our feeble frame:
He knows what sore temptations mean;
For he has felt the same.

He, in the days of feeble flesh,
Poured out his cries and tears;
And in his measure feels afresh
What every member bears.

Then let our humble faith address
His mercy and his power:
We shall obtain delivering grace
In the distressing hour.

LOWELL. L. M.
Maestoso. *From a* RUSSIAN MELODY.

87. Now let our souls, on wings sublime,
Rise from the vanities of time,
Draw back the parting veil, and see
The glories of eternity.

Shall aught beguile us on the road
While we are walking back to God?
For strangers into life we come;
And dying is but going home.

Welcome, sweet hour of full discharge,
That sets our longing souls at large,
Unbinds our chains, breaks up our cell,
And gives us with our God to dwell!

To dwell with God, to feel his love,
Is the full heaven enjoyed above;
And the sweet expectation now
Is the young dawn of heaven below.

88. Ye nations round the earth, rejoice
Before the Lord, your sovereign King;
Serve him with cheerful heart and voice;
With all your tongues his glory sing.

The Lord is God; 'tis he alone
Doth life and breath and being give:
We are his work, and not our own;
The sheep that on his pastures live.

Enter his gates with songs of joy;
With praises to his courts repair;
And make it your divine employ
To pay your thanks and honors there.

The Lord is good; the Lord is kind;
Great is his grace, his mercy sure;
And the whole race of man shall find
His truth from age to age endure.

Songs for Home-Worship.

LOVING-KINDNESS. L. M.

89.
So let our lips and lives express
The holy gospel we profess;
So let our works and virtues shine,
To prove the doctrine all divine.

Thus shall we best proclaim abroad
The honors of our Saviour God,
When his salvation reigns within,
And grace subdues the power of sin.

Our flesh and sense must be denied,
Passion and envy, lust and pride;
While justice, temperance, truth, and love
Our inward piety approve.

Religion bears our spirits up,
While we expect that blessed hope,
The bright appearing of the Lord;
And faith stands leaning on his word.

90.
Awake, my soul! and with the sun
Thy daily stage of duty run;
Shake off dull sloth, and joyful rise
To pay thy morning sacrifice.

Glory to Thee, who safe hast kept,
And hast refreshed me while I slept;
Grant, Lord, when I from death shall wake,
I may of endless life partake.

Lord, I my vows to thee renew:
Scatter my sins as morning dew;
Guard my first springs of thought and will,
And with thyself my spirit fill.

Direct, control, suggest, this day,
All I design or do or say;
That all my powers, with all their might,
In thy sole glory may unite.

HOME. 11s.

91.
I am weary of straying; oh! fain would I rest
In that far-distant land of the pure and the blest,
Where sin can no longer its blandishments spread,
And tears and temptations forever have fled.

I am weary of hoping where hope is untrue,
As fair, but as fleeting, as morning's bright dew:
I long for that land whose blest promise alone
Is changeless and sure as eternity's throne.

I am weary of loving what passes away;
The sweetest, the dearest, alas! may not stay:
I long for that land where these partings are o'er,
And death and the tomb can divide hearts no more.

I am weary, my Saviour, of grieving thy love:
Oh! when shall I rest in thy presence above?
I am weary; but, oh! let me never repine [mine.
While thy word and thy love and thy promise are

92.
'Mid scenes of confusion, and creature complaints,
How sweet to my soul is communion with saints;
To find at the banquet of mercy there's room,
And feel in the presence of Jesus at home!

Sweet bonds that unite all the children of peace,
And thrice-precious Jesus, whose love cannot cease!
Though oft from thy presence in sadness I roam,
I long to behold thee in glory at home.

While here in the valley of conflict I stay,
Oh! give me submission, and strength as my day:
In all my afflictions, to thee would I come,
Rejoicing in hope of my glorious home.

I long, dearest Lord, in thy beauty to shine;
No more as an exile in sorrow to pine;
And in thy dear image arise from the tomb,
With glorified millions to praise thee at home.

Songs for Home-Worship.

SHIRLAND. S. M. — Stanley.

93. How beauteous are their feet
 Who stand on Zion's hill;
Who bring salvation on their tongues,
 And words of peace reveal!

How happy are our ears
 That hear this joyful sound,
Which kings and prophets waited for,
 And sought, but never found!

How blessed are our eyes,
 That see this heavenly light!
Prophets and kings desired it long,
 But died without the sight.

The Lord makes bare his arm
 Through all the earth abroad:
Let every nation now behold
 Their Saviour and their God.

94. Welcome, sweet day of rest,
 That saw the Lord arise!
Welcome to this reviving breast
 And these rejoicing eyes!

The King himself comes near,
 And feasts his saints to-day:
Here we may sit, and see him here,
 And love and praise and pray.

One day amidst the place
 Where my dear God has been
Is sweeter than ten thousand days
 Of pleasurable sin.

My willing soul would stay
 In such a frame as this,
And sit, and sing herself away
 To everlasting bliss.

WINDHAM. L. M. — Daniel Read.

95. A broken heart, my God, my King,
Is all the sacrifice I bring:
The God of grace will ne'er despise
A broken heart for sacrifice.

My soul lies humbled in the dust,
And owns thy dreadful sentence just:
Look down, O Lord! with pitying eye,
And save the soul condemned to die.

Then will I teach the world thy ways;
Sinners shall learn thy sovereign grace:
I'll lead them to my Saviour's blood,
And they shall praise a pardoning God.

Oh, may thy love inspire my tongue!
Salvation shall be all my song:
And all my powers shall join to bless
The Lord, my strength and righteousness.

96. How blest the sacred tie that binds,
In union sweet, according minds!
How swift the heavenly course they run
Whose hearts and faith and hopes are one!

To each the soul of each how dear!
What jealous care! what holy fear!
How doth the generous flame within
Refine from earth, and cleanse from sin!

Together oft they seek the place
Where God reveals his awful face:
How high, how strong, their raptures swell,
There's none but kindred minds can tell.

Nor shall the glowing flame expire
'Mid nature's drooping, sickening fire:
Soon shall they meet in realms above,
A heaven of joy, because of love.

Songs for Home-Worship.

DEPARTING. L. M.

97.
I send the joys of earth away:
  Away, ye tempters of the mind,
False as the smooth, deceitful sea,
  And empty as the whistling wind!

Lord, I adore thy matchless grace,
  Which warned me of that dark abyss;
Which drew me from those treacherous seas,
  And bade me seek superior bliss.

Now to the shining realms above
  I stretch my hands, and glance my eyes:
Oh for the pinions of a dove
  To bear me to the upper skies!

There, from the bosom of my God,
  Oceans of endless pleasure roll:
There would I fix my last abode,
  And drown the sorrows of my soul.

98.
Great God! to thee my evening song
  With humble gratitude I raise:
Oh! let thy mercy tune my tongue,
  And fill my heart with lively praise.

My days, unclouded as they pass,
  And every gently-rolling hour,
Are monuments of wondrous grace,
  And witness to thy love and power.

Seal my forgiveness in the blood
  Of Jesus; his dear name alone
I plead for pardon, gracious God!
  And kind acceptance at thy throne.

Let this blest hope mine eyelids close;
  With sleep refresh my feeble frame:
Safe in thy care may I repose,
  And wake with praises to thy name!

CHIMES. C. M.   Dr. Lowell Mason.

99.
To our Redeemer's glorious name
  Awake the sacred song;
Oh, may his love — immortal flame! —
  Tune every heart and tongue!

His love what mortal thought can reach,
  What mortal tongue display?
Imagination's utmost stretch
  In wonder dies away.

Dear Lord, while we, adoring, pay
  Our humble thanks to thee,
May every heart with rapture say,
  "The Saviour died for me!"

Oh, may the sweet, the blissful theme
  Fill every heart and tongue,
Till strangers love thy charming name,
  And join the sacred song!

100.
Lord, at thy table I behold
  The wonders of thy grace,
But most of all admire that I
  Should find a welcome place.

What strange, surprising grace is this,
  That such a soul has room!
My Saviour takes me by the hand;
  My Jesus bids me come.

Ye saints below, and hosts of heaven,
  In praise join all your powers;
No theme is like redeeming love;
  No Saviour is like ours.

Had I ten thousand hearts, dear Lord,
  I'd give them all to thee;
Had I ten thousand tongues, they all
  Should join the harmony.

Songs for Home-Worship.

HEBER. C. M. KINGSLEY.

101. How honored is the sacred place
Where we adoring stand!—
Zion, the glory of the earth,
And beauty of the land.

Lift up the everlasting gates;
The doors wide open fling:
Enter, ye nations that obey
The statutes of our King!

Here shall you taste unmingled joys,
And live in perfect peace,—
You who have known Jehovah's name,
And ventured on his grace.

Trust in the Lord, forever trust,
And banish all your fears:
Strength in the Lord Jehovah dwells,
Eternal as his years.

102. There is an eye that never sleeps
Beneath the wing of night;
There is an ear that never shuts
When sink the beams of light;

There is an arm that never tires
When human strength gives way;
There is a love that never fails
When earthly loves decay.

But there's a power which man can wield
When mortal aid is vain,
That eye, that arm, that love, to reach,
That listening ear to gain.

That power is prayer, which soars on high,
Through Jesus, to the throne;
And moves the hand which moves the world,
To bring salvation down.

THATCHER. S. M. WILLIAMS.

103. Oh! cease, my wandering soul,
On restless wing to roam:
All this wide world, to either pole,
Has not for thee a home.

Behold the ark of God!
Behold the open door!
Oh! haste to gain that dear abode;
And roam, my soul, no more.

There safe thou shalt abide,
There sweet shall be thy rest,
And, every longing satisfied,
With full salvation blest.

Then cease, my wandering soul,
On restless wing to roam:
All this wide world, to either pole,
Has not for thee a home.

104. I love thy kingdom, Lord,
The house of thine abode;
The Church our blest Redeemer saved
With his own precious blood.

I love thy Church, O God!
Her walls before thee stand,
Dear as the apple of thine eye,
And graven on thy hand.

For her my tears shall fall,
For her my prayers ascend;
To her my cares and toils be given,
Till toils and cares shall end.

Sure as thy truth shall last,
To Zion shall be given
The brightest glories earth can yield,
And brighter bliss of heaven.

Songs for Home-Worship.

COWPER. C. M. — Dr. Lowell Mason.

105. Blest hour, when righteous souls shall meet,
Shall meet to part no more,
And with celestial welcome greet
On an immortal shore !

The parent finds his long-lost child ;
Brothers on brothers gaze :
The tear of resignation mild
Is changed to joy and praise.

Each tender tie, dissolved with pain,
With endless bliss is crowned :
All that was dead revives again ;
All that was lost is found.

Congenial minds, arrayed in light,
High thoughts shall interchange ;
Nor cease, with ever-new delight,
On wings of love to range.

106. There is a glorious world of light
Above the starry sky,
Where saints departed, clothed in white,
Adore the Lord most high.

And hark ! amid the sacred songs
Those heavenly voices raise,
Ten thousand thousand infant tongues
Unite in perfect praise.

Soon will our earthly race be run,
Our mortal frame decay :
Parents and children, one by one,
Must die, and pass away.

Great God ! impress this solemn thought
To-day on every breast :
May both the teachers and the taught
Be found among the blest !

ARLINGTON. C. M. — Dr. Arne.

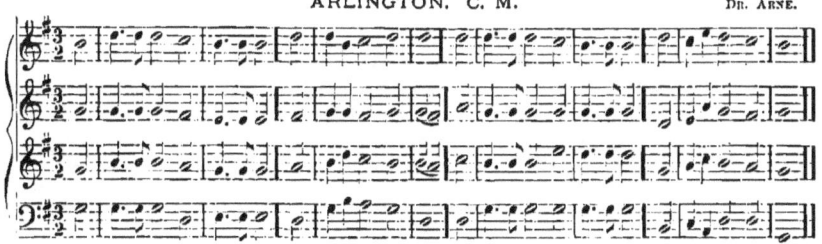

107. This is the day the Lord hath made ;
He calls the hours his own :
Let heaven rejoice, let earth be glad,
And praise surround the throne.

Hosanna to the anointed King,
To David's holy Son !
Help us, O Lord ! descend, and bring
Salvation from thy throne.

Blest be the Lord, who comes to men
With messages of grace ;
Who comes in God his Father's name
To save our sinful race.

Hosanna in the highest strains
The Church on earth can raise !
The highest heaven, in which he reigns,
Shall give him nobler praise.

108. O Thou from whom all goodness flows !
I lift my soul to thee :
In all my sorrows, conflicts, woes,
O Lord ! remember me.

When trials sore obstruct my way,
And ills I cannot flee,
Oh ! let my strength be as my day :
Dear Lord, remember me.

When in the solemn hour of death
I wait thy just decree,
Be this the prayer of my last breath,
" Now, Lord, remember me."

And when before thy throne I stand,
And lift my soul to thee,
Then with the saints at thy right hand,
O Lord ! remember me.

Songs for Home-Worship.

ST. JOHN'S. L. M.

109. Sweet is the memory of thy grace,
My God, my heavenly King:
Let age to age thy righteousness
In sounds of glory sing.

God reigns on high, but ne'er confines
His goodness to the skies:
Through the whole earth his bounty shines,
And every want supplies.

How kind are thy compassions, Lord!
How slow thine anger moves!
But soon he sends his pardoning word
To cheer the souls he loves.

Sweet is the memory of thy grace,
My God, my heavenly King:
Let age to age thy righteousness
In sounds of glory sing.

110. How bright these glorious spirits shine!
Whence all their white array?
How came they to the blissful seats
Of everlasting day?

Lo! these are they from sufferings great
Who came to realms of light,
And in the blood of Christ have washed
Those robes which shine so bright.

His presence fills each heart with joy;
Tunes every voice to sing:
By day, by night, the sacred courts
With glad hosannas ring.

In pastures green he'll lead his flock,
Where living streams appear;
And God, the Lord, from every eye
Shall wipe away each tear.

WEBB. 7s and 6s. G. J. WEBB.

111. The morning light is breaking;
The darkness disappears:
The sons of earth are waking
To penitential tears.

Each breeze that sweeps the ocean
Brings tidings from afar
Of nations in commotion,
Prepared for Zion's war.

Rich dews of grace come o'er us
In many a gentle shower,
And brighter scenes before us
Are opening every hour.

Each cry to heaven going
Abundant answer brings;
And heavenly gales are blowing,
With peace upon their wings.

112. See heathen nations bending
Before the God of love,
And thousand hearts ascending
In gratitude above!

While sinners, now confessing,
The gospel's call obey,
And seek a Saviour's blessing,
A nation in a day.

Blest river of salvation,
Pursue thy onward way;
Flow thou to every nation,
Nor in thy richness stay:

Stay not till all the lowly
Triumphant reach their home;
Stay not till all the holy
Proclaim the Lord is come.

Songs for Home-Worship.

NAOMI. C. M.
Dr. Lowell Mason, *by permission.*

113.
Return, O wanderer! now return,
And seek thy Father's face:
These new desires which in thee burn
Are kindled by his grace.

Return, O wanderer! now return:
He hears thy humble sigh,
He sees thy softened spirit mourn,
When no one else is nigh.

Return, O wanderer! now return;
Thy Saviour bids thee live:
Go to his bleeding feet, and learn
How freely he'll forgive.

Return, O wanderer! now return,
And wipe the falling tear:
Thy Father calls; no longer mourn;
His love invites thee near.

114.
Great Father of each perfect gift,
Behold, thy servants wait;
With longing eyes and lifted hands
We flock around thy gate.

Oh! shed abroad that choicest gift,
Thy Spirit from above,
To cheer our eyes with sacred light,
And fire our hearts with love.

With speedy flight may he descend,
And solid comfort bring,
And o'er our languid souls extend
His all-reviving wing.

Blest Earnest of eternal joy,
Declare our sins forgiven,
And bear with energy divine
Our raptured thoughts to heaven.

LABAN. S. M.
Allegro Vigoroso.

115.
Our heavenly Father, hear
The prayer we offer now:
Thy name be hallowed far and near;
To thee all nations bow.

Thy kingdom come; thy will
On earth be done in love,
As saints and seraphim fulfil
Thy perfect law above.

Our daily bread supply,
While by thy Word we live;
The guilt of our iniquity
Forgive as we forgive.

Thine, then, forever be
Glory and power divine:
The sceptre, throne, and majesty
Of heaven and earth are thine.

116.
Like sheep we went astray,
And broke the fold of God;
Each wandering in a different way,
But all the downward road.

How glorious was the grace
When Christ sustained the stroke!
His life and blood the Shepherd pays,
A ransom for the flock.

But God shall raise his head
O'er all the sons of men,
And make him see a numerous seed
To recompense his pain.

"I'll give him," saith the Lord,
"A portion with the strong:
He shall possess a large reward,
And hold his honors long."

Songs for Home-Worship.

Slowly.   AVON. C. M.   Scottish Tune.

117.
Come, let us to the Lord our God
With contrite hearts return:
Our God is gracious, nor will leave
The desolate to mourn.

Our hearts, if God we seek to know,
Shall know him, and rejoice:
His coming like the morn shall be;
Like morning songs his voice.

As dew upon the tender herb,
Diffusing fragrance round;
As showers that usher in the spring,
And cheer the thirsty ground:

So shall his presence bless our souls,
And shed a joyful light:
That hallowed morn shall chase away
The sorrows of the night.

118.
Bright Source of everlasting love,
To thee our souls we raise,
And to thy sovereign bounty rear
A monument of praise.

Thy mercy gilds the path of life
With every cheering ray;
Kindly restrains the rising tear,
Or wipes that tear away.

The widow's heart shall sing for joy;
The orphan shall be fed:
The hungering soul we'll gladly point
To Christ, the living bread.

Thus what our heavenly Father gave
Shall we as freely give;
Thus copy Him who lived to save,
And died that we might live.

ANTIOCH. C. M.   *Arranged by* L. Mason.

119.
Joy to the world, the Lord is come!
Let earth receive her King;
Let every heart prepare him room,
And heaven and nature sing.

Joy to the earth, the Saviour reigns!
Let men their songs employ;
While fields and floods, rocks, hills, and plains,
Repeat the sounding joy.

No more let sins and sorrows grow,
Nor thorns infest the ground:
He comes to make his blessings flow
Far as the curse is found.

He rules the world with truth and grace,
And makes the nations prove
The glories of his righteousness,
And wonders of his love.

120.
O all ye lands! rejoice in God;
Sing praises to his name:
Let all the earth, with one accord,
His wondrous acts proclaim.

And let his faithful servants tell
How, by redeeming love,
Their souls are saved from death and hell,
To share the joys above,—

Tell how the Holy Spirit's grace
Forbids their feet to slide;
And, as they run the Christian race,
Vouchsafes to be their guide.

Oh, then, rejoice, and shout for joy,
Ye ransomed of the Lord!
Be grateful praise your sweet employ,
His presence your reward.

Songs for Home-Worship.

HENRY. C. M.
S. B. POND.

121. O God! my heart is fully bent
To magnify thy name:
My tongue, with cheerful songs of praise,
Shall celebrate thy fame.

Awake, my lute! nor thou, my harp!
Thy warbling notes delay,
While I, with early hymns of joy,
Prevent the dawning day.

To all the listening tribes, O Lord!
Thy wonders I will tell,
And to those nations sing thy praise
That round about us dwell;

Because thy mercy's boundless height
The highest heaven transcends,
And far beyond the aspiring clouds
Thy faithful truth extends.

122. A glory gilds the sacred page,
Majestic, like the sun:
It gives a light to every age;
It gives, but borrows none.

The hand that gave it still supplies
The gracious light and heat:
Its truths upon the nations rise;
They rise, but never set.

Let everlasting thanks be thine
For such a bright display
As makes a world of darkness shine
With beams of heavenly day.

My soul rejoices to pursue
The steps of Him I love.
Till glory breaks upon my view
In brighter worlds above.

ROSSINI. C. M.

123. Praise to the radiant Source of bliss,
Who gives the blind their sight,
And scatters round their wondering eyes
A flood of sacred light.

In paths unknown he leads them on
To his divine abode;
And shows new miracles of grace
Through all the heavenly road.

The ways all rugged and perplexed
He renders smooth and straight,
And strengthens every feeble knee
To march to Zion's gate.

Through all the path I'll sing his name
Till I the mount ascend
Where toils and storms are known no more,
And anthems never end.

124. Happy the home when God is there,
And love fills every breast;
Where one their wish, and one their prayer,
And one their heavenly rest.

Happy the home where Jesus' name
Is sweet to every ear;
Where children early lisp his fame,
And parents hold him dear.

Happy the home where prayer is heard,
And praise is wont to rise;
Where parents love the sacred Word,
And live but for the skies.

Lord! let us in our home agree
This blessed peace to gain:
Unite our hearts in love to thee,
And love to all will reign.

Songs for Home-Worship.

DEDHAM. C. M.

125. Long as I live I'll bless thy name,
My King, my God of love:
My work and joy shall be the same
In the bright world above.

Great is the Lord, his power unknown;
Oh! let his praise be great:
I'll sing the honors of thy throne,
Thy works of grace repeat.

Thy grace shall dwell upon my tongue;
And, while my lips rejoice,
The men who hear my sacred song
Shall join their cheerful voice.

Fathers to sons shall teach thy name,
And children learn thy ways;
Ages to come thy truth proclaim,
And nations sound thy praise.

126. Thou must go forth alone, my soul,
Thou must go forth alone,
To other scenes, to other worlds,
That mortal hath not known.

Thou must go forth alone, my soul,
To tread the narrow vale;
But He whose word is sure hath said
His mercy shall not fail.

Thou must go forth alone, my soul,
To meet thy God above.
But shrink not: he has said, my soul,
He is a God of love.

His rod and staff shall comfort thee
Across the dreary road,
Till thou shalt join the blessed ones
In heaven's serene abode.

DITCHLING. C. M.

127. There is a land of pure delight,
Where saints immortal reign:
Infinite day excludes the night,
And pleasures banish pain.

There everlasting spring abides,
And never-withering flowers:
Death, like a narrow sea, divides
This heavenly land from ours.

Oh! could we make our doubts remove,
Those gloomy doubts that rise,
And see the Canaan that we love
With unbeclouded eyes;

Could we but climb where Moses stood,
And view the landscape o'er,—
Not Jordan's stream nor death's cold flood
Should fright us from the shore.

128. Remember thy Creator now
In these thy youthful days:
He will accept thy earliest vow,
And listen to thy praise.

Remember thy Creator now,
And seek him while he's near:
For evil days will come, when thou
Shalt find no comfort near.

Remember thy Creator now;
His willing servant be:
Then, when thy head in death shall bow,
He will remember thee.

Almighty God! our hearts incline
Thy heavenly voice to hear:
Let all our future days be thine,
Devoted to thy fear.

Songs for Home-Worship.

Allegro. GROTON. C. M. Ch. Zeuner.

129. Ye hosts of heaven, ye mighty ones,
Ascribe with one accord
The strength, the power, the majesty,
To your almighty Lord.

Give glory to his holy name,
And honor him alone;
In beauty meet of holiness
Approach his lofty throne.

Jehovah's voice of majesty
Is on the waters wide;
The God of glory thundereth,
And on the seas doth ride.

Jehovah sits upon the floods,
And tempests rage in vain;
Jehovah sits as sovereign King,
And evermore shall reign.

130. Oh! praise the Lord; for he is good;
In him we rest obtain;
His mercy has through ages stood,
And ever shall remain.

Let all the people of the Lord
His praises spread around;
Let them his grace and love record
Who have salvation found.

Now let the east in him rejoice,
The west its tribute bring,
The north and south lift up their voice
In honor of their King.

Oh! praise the Lord; for he is good;
In him we rest obtain;
His mercy has through ages stood,
And ever shall remain.

MARLOW. C. M.

131. Since all the varying scenes of time
God's watchful eye surveys,
Oh! who so wise to choose our lot,
Or to appoint our ways?

Good when he gives, supremely good;
Nor less when he denies:
E'en crosses from his sovereign hand
Are blessings in disguise.

Why should we doubt a Father's love,
So constant and so kind?
To his unerring, gracious will
Be every wish resigned.

In thy fair book of life divine,
My God, inscribe my name:
There let it fill some humble place
Beneath my Lord, the Lamb.

132. Jehovah, God! thy gracious power
On every hand we see;
Oh, may the blessings of each hour
Lead all our thoughts to thee!

If on the wings of morn we speed
To earth's remotest bound,
Thy hand will there our footsteps lead,
Thy love our path surround.

Thy power is in the ocean-deeps,
And reaches to the skies;
Thine eye of mercy never sleeps;
Thy goodness never dies.

From morn till noon, till latest eve,
Thy hand, O God! we see;
And all the blessings we receive
Proceed alone from thee.

Songs for Home-Worship.

SWANWICK. C. M.

133.
Arise, ye people! and adore;
Exulting strike the chord:
Let all the earth, from shore to shore,
Confess the almighty Lord.

Glad shouts aloud, wide echoing round,
The ascending God proclaim;
The angelic choir respond the sound,
And shake creation's frame.

They sing of death and hell o'erthrown
In that triumphant hour;
And God exalts his conquering Son
To his right hand of power.

Oh, shout, ye people! and adore;
Exulting strike the chord:
Let all the earth, from shore to shore,
Confess the almighty Lord.

134.
Witness, ye men and angels, now
Before the Lord we speak;
To him we make our solemn vow,—
A vow we dare not break,—

That, long as life itself shall last,
Ourselves to Christ we yield;
Nor from his cause will we depart,
Or ever quit the field.

We trust not in our native strength,
But on his grace rely,
That with returning wants the Lord
Will all our need supply.

Oh! guide our doubtful feet aright,
And keep us in thy ways;
And, while we turn our vows to prayers,
Turn thou our prayers to praise.

LISBON. S. M.

135.
My spirit on thy care,
Blest Saviour, I recline:
Thou wilt not leave me to despair;
For thou art love divine.

In thee I place my trust;
On thee I calmly rest:
I know thee good, I know thee just,
And count thy choice the best.

Whate'er events betide,
Thy will they all perform:
Safe on thy breast my head I hide,
Nor fear the coming storm.

Let good or ill befall,
It must be good for me,
Secure of having thee in all,
Of having all in thee.

136.
My soul, be on thy guard:
Ten thousand foes arise;
The hosts of Sin are pressing hard
To draw thee from the skies.

Oh! watch and fight and pray;
The battle ne'er give o'er;
Renew it boldly every day,
And help divine implore.

Ne'er think the victory won,
Nor lay thine armor down:
Thy arduous work will not be done
Till thou obtain thy crown.

Fight on, my soul, till death
Shall bring thee to thy God;
He'll take thee, at thy parting breath,
Up to his blest abode.

Songs for Home-Worship.

OLMUTZ. S. M. — Gregorian.

137.
To God, the only wise,
 Our Saviour and our King,
Let all the saints below the skies
 Their humble praises bring.

'Tis his almighty love,
 His counsel, and his care,
Preserves us safe from sin and death,
 And every hurtful snare.

He will present our souls
 Unblemished and complete
Before the glory of his face
 With joys divinely great.

To our Redeemer, God,
 Wisdom with power belongs,
Immortal crowns of majesty,
 And everlasting songs.

138.
Jesus, who knows full well
 The heart of every saint,
Invites us all our griefs to tell;
 To pray, and never faint.

He bows his gracious ear;
 We never plead in vain:
Yet we must wait till he appear;
 And pray, and pray again.

Jesus, the Lord, will hear
 His chosen when they cry:
Yes, though he may a while forbear,
 He'll help them from on high.

Then let us earnest be,
 And never faint in prayer:
He loves our importunity,
 And makes our cause his care.

OVA. C. M. — Arranged from Mozart.

Moderato.

139.
My Saviour! my almighty Friend!
 When I begin thy praise,
Where will the growing numbers end, —
 The numbers of thy grace?

Thou art my everlasting trust;
 Thy goodness I adore:
And, since I knew thy graces first,
 I speak thy glories more.

My feet shall travel all the length
 Of the celestial road;
And march, with courage in thy strength,
 To see my Father, God.

Awake, awake, my tuneful powers!
 With this delightful song
I'll entertain the darkest hours,
 Nor think the season long.

140.
Eternal Wisdom! thee we praise;
 Thee the creation sings:
With thy loved name rocks, hills, and seas,
 And heaven's high palace, rings.

Thy hand — how wide it spread the sky!
 How glorious to behold!
Tinged with a blue of heavenly dye,
 And starred with sparkling gold.

Infinite strength and equal skill
 Shine forth the world abroad,
Our souls with vast amazement fill,
 And speak the builder, God.

But still the wonders of thy grace
 Our softer passions move:
Pity divine in Jesus' face
 We see, adore, and love.

Songs for Home-Worship.

WIRGMAN. 7s.
Molto Soave.

141.
Praise the Lord, his glories show,
Saints within his courts below,
Angels round his throne above,
All that see and share his love.

Earth to heaven, and heaven to earth,
Tell his wonders, sing his worth;
Age to age, and shore to shore,
Praise him, praise him, evermore.

Praise the Lord, his mercies trace;
Praise his providence and grace, —
All that he for man hath done,
All he sends us through his Son.

Strings and voices, hands and hearts,
In the concert bear your parts;
All that breathe, your Lord adore;
Praise him, praise him, evermore.

142.
Softly now the light of day
Fades upon my sight away;
Free from care, from labor free,
Lord, I would commune with thee.

Thou, whose all-pervading eye
Nought escapes, without, within,
Pardon each infirmity,
Open fault, and secret sin.

Soon for me the light of day
Shall forever pass away:
Then, from sin and sorrow free,
Take me, Lord, to dwell with thee.

Thou who, sinless, yet hast known
All of man's infirmity,
Then from thine eternal throne,
Jesus, look with pitying eye.

NORTHFIELD. C. M.
J. INGALLS.

143.
Behold the glories of the Lamb
Amid his Father's throne!
Prepare new honors for his name,
And songs before unknown.

Let elders worship at his feet,
The Church adore around,
With vials full of odor sweet,
And harps of sweeter sound.

Now to the Lamb that once was slain
Be endless blessings paid;
Salvation, glory, joy, remain
Forever on thy head!

Thou hast redeemed our souls with blood,
Hast set the prisoners free,
Hast made us kings and priests to God;
And we shall reign with thee.

144.
Come in, thou blessed of the Lord!
Stranger nor foe art thou;
We welcome thee with warm accord,
Our friend, our brother, now.

The hand of fellowship, the heart
Of love, we offer thee;
Leaving the world, thou dost but part
From lies and vanity.

Come with us; we will do thee good
As God to us hath done:
Stand but in him as those have stood
Whose faith the victory won.

And when by turns we pass away,
And star by star grows dim,
May each, translated into day,
Be lost and found in him!

Songs for Home-Worship.

MAHALETH. C. M.

115.
My God, my Portion, and my Love,
  My everlasting All,
I've none but thee in heaven above,
  Or on this earthly ball.

How vain a toy is glittering wealth
  If once compared with thee!
Or what's my safety or my health,
  Or all my friends, to me?

Were I possessor of the earth,
  And called the stars my own,
Without thy graces and thyself,
  I were a wretch undone.

Let others stretch their arms like seas,
  And grasp in all the shore:
Grant me the visits of thy face,
  And I desire no more.

146.
Awake, ye saints! and raise your eyes,
  And lift your voices high;
Awake, and praise the sovereign love
  That shows salvation nigh.

Swift on the wings of time it flies;
  Each moment brings it near:
Then welcome, each declining day!
  Welcome, each closing year!

Not many years their round shall run,
  Not many mornings rise,
Ere all its glories stand revealed
  To our admiring eyes.

Ye wheels of Nature, speed your course!
  Ye mortal powers, decay!
Fast as ye bring the night of death,
  Ye bring eternal day.

DENFIELD. C. M.

147.
Dear Father, to thy mercy-seat
  My soul for shelter flies:
'Tis here I find a safe retreat
  When storms and tempests rise.

My cheerful hope can never die,
  If thou, my God, art near:
Thy grace can raise my comforts high,
  And banish every fear.

My great Protector, and my Lord,
  Thy constant aid impart:
Oh! let thy kind, thy gracious word
  Sustain my trembling heart.

Oh! never let my soul remove
  From this divine retreat:
Still let me trust thy power and love,
  And dwell beneath thy feet.

148.
Oh! 'twas a joyful sound to hear
  Our tribes devoutly say,
"Up, Israel! to the temple haste,
  And keep your festal day!"

At Salem's courts we must appear
  With our assembled powers,
In strong and beauteous order ranged,
  Like her united towers.

Oh! pray we, then, for Salem's peace;
  For they shall prosperous be,
Thou holy city of our God,
  Who bear true love to thee.

May Peace within thy sacred walls
  A constant guest be found!
With plenty and prosperity
  Thy palaces be crowned!

Songs for Home-Worship.

ROCKVILLE. C. M.

Allegretto. Ch. Zeuner.

149. Oh for a shout of sacred joy
To God, the sovereign King!
Let every land their tongues employ,
And hymns of triumph sing.

While angels shout and praise their King,
Let mortals learn their strains;
Let all the earth his honor sing;
O'er all the earth he reigns.

Rehearse his praise with awe profound:
Let knowledge lead the song;
Nor mock him with a solemn sound
Upon a thoughtless tongue.

Oh for a shout of sacred joy
To God, the sovereign King!
Let every land their tongues employ,
And hymns of triumph sing.

150. Through endless years thou art the same,
O thou eternal God!
Ages to come shall know thy name,
And tell thy works abroad.

The strong foundations of the earth
Of old by thee were laid;
By thee the beauteous arch of heaven
With matchless skill was made.

Soon shall this goodly frame of things,
Formed by thy powerful hand,
Be, like a vesture, laid aside,
And changed at thy command.

But thy perfections all divine,
Eternal as thy days,
Through everlasting ages shine
With undiminished rays.

THAXTED. C. M.

Beethoven.

151. Come, let us lift our joyful eyes
Up to the courts above,
And smile to see our Father there
Upon a throne of love.

Come, let us bow before his feet,
And venture near the Lord :
No fiery cherubs guard his seat,
Nor double-flaming sword.

The peaceful gates of heavenly bliss
Are opened by the Son ;
High let us raise our notes of praise,
And reach the almighty throne.

To thee ten thousand thanks we bring,
Great Advocate on high ;
And glory to the eternal King,
Who lays his anger by.

152. 'Tis by thy strength the mountains stand,
God of eternal power :
The sea grows calm at thy command,
And tempests cease to roar.

Thy morning light and evening shade
Successive comforts bring:
Thy plenteous fruits make harvest glad ;
Thy flowers adorn the spring.

Seasons and times, and moons and hours,
Heaven, earth, and air, are thine :
When clouds distil in fruitful showers,
The author is divine.

Thy showers the thirsty furrows fill,
And ranks of corn appear ;
Thy ways abound with blessings still ;
Thy goodness crowns the year.

Songs for Home-Worship.

HOLBEIN. C. M.

153. Lord, when we bend before thy throne,
And our confessions pour,
Teach us to feel the sins we own,
And hate what we deplore.

Our broken spirit pitying see;
True penitence impart;
Then let a kindling glance from thee
Beam hope upon the heart.

When we disclose our wants in prayer,
May we our wills resign,
And not a thought our bosoms share
Which is not wholly thine!

May faith each meek petition fill,
And waft it to the skies,
And teach our hearts 'tis Goodness still
That grants it or denies!

154. Oh! happy is the man that hears
Instruction's warning voice;
And who celestial Wisdom makes
His early, only choice.

For she hath treasures greater far
Than east and west unfold;
And her rewards more precious are
Than all their stores of gold.

She guides the young with innocence,
In Pleasure's paths to tread:
A crown of glory she bestows
Upon the hoary head.

According as her labors rise,
So her rewards increase;
Her ways are ways of pleasantness,
And all her paths are peace.

GEER. C. M.

155. Amid the splendors of thy state,
O God! thy love appears,
Soft as the radiance of the moon
Among a thousand stars.

In all thy doctrines and commands,
Thy counsels and designs,
In every work thy hands have framed,
Thy love supremely shines.

Sinai, in clouds and smoke and fire,
Thunders thine awful name;
But Zion sings, in melting notes,
The honors of the Lamb.

Angels and men the news proclaim
Through earth and heaven above;
And all, with holy transport, sing
That God the Lord is love.

156. Early, my God, without delay,
I haste to seek thy face:
My thirsty spirit faints away
Without thy cheering grace.

So pilgrims on the scorching sand,
Beneath a burning sky,
Long for a cooling stream at hand;
And they must drink, or die.

I've seen thy glory and thy power
Through all thy temple shine;
My God, repeat that heavenly hour,
That vision so divine!

Not life itself, with all its joys,
Can my best passions move,
Or raise so high my cheerful voice,
As thy forgiving love.

Songs for Home-Worship.

WEST POINT. S. M.   C. W. BEAMES.

157.
Come, we that love the Lord,
And let our joys be known;
Join in a song with sweet accord,
And thus surround the throne.

Let those refuse to sing
That never knew our God;
But children of the heavenly King
May speak their joys abroad.

The hill of Zion yields
A thousand sacred sweets
Before we reach the heavenly fields
Or walk the golden streets.

Then let our songs abound,
And every tear be dry:
We're marching through Immanuel's ground
To fairer worlds on high.

158.
Oh for the peace of those
Who slumber in the Lord!
Oh, be like theirs my last repose,
Like theirs my last reward!

Their bodies in the ground
In silent hope may lie
Till the last trumpet's joyful sound
Shall call them to the sky.

Their ransomed spirits soar
On wings of faith and love
To meet the Saviour they adore,
And reign with him above.

With us their names shall live
Through long succeeding years,
Embalmed with all our hearts can give,
Our praises and our tears.

FANE. C. M.

Andante Grazioso. Count six moderately for a measure.   P. WINTER.

159.
I know that my Redeemer lives;
He lives who once was dead:
To me in grief he comfort gives;
With peace he crowns my head.

He lives triumphant o'er the grave,
At God's right hand on high,
My ransomed soul to keep and save,
To bless and glorify.

He lives that I may also live,
And now his grace proclaim;
He lives that I may honor give
To his most holy name.

Let strains of heavenly music rise,
While all their anthem sing
To Christ, my precious Sacrifice,
And ever-living King.

160.
When all thy mercies, O my God!
My rising soul surveys,
Transported with the view, I'm lost
In wonder, love, and praise.

Ten thousand thousand precious gifts
My daily thanks employ;
Nor is the least a cheerful heart,
That tastes those gifts with joy.

Through every period of my life,
Thy goodness I'll pursue;
And after death, in distant worlds,
The glorious theme renew.

Through all eternity, to thee
A joyful song I'll raise;
But, oh! eternity's too short
To utter all thy praise.

Songs for Home-Worship.

SILVER STREET. S. M.   I. SMITH.

161.
Awake! and sing the song
Of Moses and the Lamb ;
Tune every heart and every tongue
To praise the Saviour's name.

Soon shall we hear him say,
"Ye blessed children, come !"
Soon will he call us hence away
To our eternal home.

Soon shall our raptured tongue
His endless praise proclaim,
And sweeter voices tune the song
Of Moses and the Lamb.

Sing, till we feel our hearts
Ascending with our tongues ;
Sing, till the love of sin departs,
And grace inspires our songs.

162.
My God, my Life, my Love,
To thee, to thee, I call :
I cannot live if thou remove ;
For thou art all in all.

To thee, and thee alone,
The angels owe their bliss :
They sit around thy gracious throne,
And dwell where Jesus is.

Nor earth, nor all the sky,
Can one delight afford,
No, not a drop of real joy,
Without thy presence, Lord.

Thou art the sea of love,
Where all my pleasures roll,
The circle where my passions move,
And centre of my soul.

WALTON. C. M.

163.
Once more, my soul, the rising day
Salutes my waking eyes;
Once more, my voice, thy tribute pay
To Him who rules the skies.

Night unto night his name repeats,
The day renews the sound,
Wide as the heavens on which he sits
To turn the seasons round.

'Tis he supports my mortal frame :
My tongue shall speak his praise :
My sins would rouse his wrath to flame ;
And yet his wrath delays.

Great God ! let all my hours be thine
While I enjoy the light ;
Then shall my sun in smiles decline,
And bring a pleasant night.

164.
Let every mortal ear attend,
And every heart rejoice :
The trumpet of the gospel sounds
With an inviting voice.

Eternal Wisdom has prepared
A soul-reviving feast,
And bids your longing appetites
The rich provision taste.

Rivers of love and mercy here
In a rich ocean join :
Salvation in abundance flows
Like floods of milk and wine.

The happy gates of gospel grace
Stand open night and day :
Lord, we are come to seek supplies,
And drive our wants away.

Songs for Home-Worship.

SELVIN. S. M.

165. Behold, the morning sun
Begins his glorious way!
His beams through all the nations run,
And life and light convey.

But, where the gospel comes,
It spreads diviner light:
It calls dead sinners from their tombs,
And gives the blind their sight.

How perfect is Thy word!
And all Thy judgments just:
Forever sure thy promise, Lord,
And men securely trust.

My gracious God, how plain
Are thy directions given!
Oh, may I never read in vain,
But find the path to heaven!

166. Give to the winds thy fears;
Hope, and be undismayed:
God hears thy sighs, and counts thy tears;
God shall lift up thy head.

Through waves, through clouds and storms,
He gently clears thy way;
Wait thou his time; so shall this night
Soon end in joyous day.

Still heavy is thy heart;
Still sink thy spirits down:
Cast off the weight; let fear depart;
Bid every care be gone.

Far, far above thy thought
His counsel shall appear
When fully He the work hath wrought
That caused thy needless fear.

NINEVEH. C. M.

167. Let saints below in concert sing
With those to glory gone;
For all the servants of our King,
In earth and heaven, are one.

One family, we dwell in him,
One church above, beneath,
Though now divided by the stream,
The narrow stream, of death.

One army of the living God,
To his command we bow;
Part of the host have crossed the flood,
And part are crossing now.

Lord Jesus, be our constant guide;
And, when the word is given,
Bid death's cold flood its waves divide,
And land us safe in heaven.

168. My God, the spring of all my joys,
The life of my delights,
The glory of my brightest days,
And comfort of my nights!

In darkest shades if he appear,
My dawning is begun;
He is my soul's sweet morning-star,
And he my rising sun.

The opening heavens around me shine
With beams of sacred bliss;
While Jesus shows his heart is mine,
And whispers I am his.

My soul would leave this heavy clay
At that transporting word,
Run up with joy the shining way
To embrace my dearest Lord.

Songs for Home-Worship.

LONDON. C. M.
Scotch Psalter.

169. In all my vast concerns with thee,
In vain my soul would try
To shun thy presence, Lord, or flee
The notice of thine eye.

My thoughts lie open to the Lord
Before they're formed within;
And, ere my lips pronounce the word,
He knows the sense I mean.

Oh wondrous knowledge, deep and high!
Where can a creature hide?
Within thy circling arms I lie,
Beset on every side.

So let thy grace surround me still,
And like a bulwark prove,
To guard my soul from every ill,
Secured by sovereign love.

170. Great God, how infinite art thou!
What worthless worms are we!
Let the whole race of creatures bow,
And pay their praise to thee.

Eternity, with all its years,
Stands present in thy view:
To thee there's nothing old appears;
Great God, there's nothing new.

Our lives through various scenes are drawn,
And vexed with trifling cares;
While thine eternal thought moves on
Thine undisturbed affairs.

Great God, how infinite art thou!
What worthless worms are we!
Let the whole race of creatures bow,
And pay their praise to thee.

PENTONVILLE. S. M.
Linley.

171. Grace!—'tis a charming sound,
Harmonious to my ear;
Heaven with the echo shall resound,
And all the earth shall hear.

Grace first contrived a way
To save rebellious man;
And all the steps that grace display
Which drew the wondrous plan.

Grace taught my wandering feet
To tread the heavenly road;
And new supplies each hour I meet,
While pressing on to God.

Grace all the work shall crown
Through everlasting days;
It lays in heaven the topmost stone,
And well deserves the praise.

172. Come, sound his praise abroad,
And hymns of glory sing:
Jehovah is the sovereign God,
The universal King.

He formed the deeps unknown;
He gave the seas their bound:
The watery worlds are all his own,
And all the solid ground.

Come, worship at his throne;
Come, bow before the Lord:
We are his work, and not our own;
He formed us by his word.

To-day attend his voice,
Nor dare provoke his rod:
Come like the people of his choice,
And own your gracious God.

Songs for Home-Worship.

HENDON. 7s.
Dr. Malan.

173.
Songs of praise the angels sang,
Heaven with hallelujahs rang,
When Jehovah's work begun;
When God spake, and it was done.

Songs of praise awoke the morn
When the Prince of peace was born;
Songs of praise arose when he
Captive led captivity.

Heaven and earth must pass away;
Songs of praise shall crown that day;
God will make new heaven and earth;
Songs of praise shall hail their birth.

Saints below, with heart and voice,
Still in songs of praise rejoice;
Learning here, by faith and love,
Songs of praise to sing above.

174.
"Christ, the Lord, is risen to-day!"
Sons of men, and angels, say.
Raise your joys and triumphs high;
Sing, ye heavens; and, earth, reply.

Love's redeeming work is done;
Fought the fight, the battle won;
Lo! our sun's eclipse is o'er;
Lo! he sets in blood no more.

Lives again our glorious King:
Where, O Death! is now thy sting?
Once he died our souls to save:
Where thy victory, boasting Grave?

Soar we now where Christ has led,
Following our exalted Head;
Made like him, like him we rise;
Ours the cross, the grave, the skies!

MIGDOL. L. M.
L. Mason.

175.
The Lord — how wondrous are his ways!
How firm his truth! how large his grace!
He takes his mercy for his throne,
And thence he makes his glories known.

Not half so high his power hath spread
The starry heavens above our head
As his rich love exceeds our praise,
Exceeds the highest hopes we raise.

Not half so far has Nature placed
The rising morning from the west
As his forgiving grace removes
The daily guilt of those he loves.

How slowly doth his wrath arise!
On swifter wings salvation flies;
Or, if he lets his anger burn,
How soon his frowns to pity turn!

176.
Thine earthly sabbaths, Lord, we love;
But there's a nobler rest above:
To that our laboring souls aspire
With ardent pangs of strong desire.

No more fatigue, no more distress;
Nor sin nor hell shall reach the place;
No groans to mingle with the songs
Which warble from immortal tongues;

No rude alarms of raging foes;
No cares to break the long repose;
No midnight shade, no clouded sun,
But sacred, high, eternal noon.

Thine earthly sabbaths, Lord, we love;
But there's a nobler rest above:
To that our laboring souls aspire
With ardent pangs of strong desire.

Songs for Home-Worship.

WELLS. L. M.
ISRAEL HOLDRAYD.

177.
Praises to Him whose love has given,
In Christ, his Son, the Light of heaven;
Who for our darkness gives us light,
And turns to day our deepest night.

Praises to Him in grace who came
To bear our woe and sin and shame;
Who lived to die, who died to rise,
The God-accepted sacrifice.

Praises to Him who sheds abroad
Within our hearts the love of God;
The Spirit of all truth and peace,
Fountain of joy and holiness.

To Father, Son, and Spirit now
The hands we lift, the knees we bow:
To thee, Jehovah, thus we raise
The sinner's endless song of praise.

178.
High in the heavens, eternal God,
Thy goodness in full glory shines:
The truth shall break through every cloud
That veils and darkens thy designs.

Forever firm thy justice stands
As mountains their foundations keep:
Wise are the wonders of thine hands;
Thy judgments are a mighty deep.

Thy providence is kind and large,
Both man and beast thy bounty share:
The whole creation is thy charge;
But saints are thy peculiar care.

My God, how excellent thy grace,
Whence all our hope and comfort springs!
The sons of Adam, in distress,
Fly to the shadow of thy wings.

PLEYEL'S HYMN. 7s.

179.
Softly fades the twilight ray
Of the holy sabbath day,
Gently as life's setting sun
When the Christian's course is run.

Night her solemn mantle spreads
O'er the earth as daylight fades:
All things tell of calm repose
At the holy sabbath's close.

Still the Spirit lingers near
Where the evening worshipper
Seeks communion with the skies,
Pressing onward to the prize.

Saviour, may our sabbaths be
Days of peace and joy in thee,
Till in heaven our souls repose,
Where the sabbath ne'er shall close!

180.
Morning breaks upon the tomb;
Jesus scatters all its gloom:
Day of triumph through the skies;
See the glorious Saviour rise!

Christians, dry your flowing tears;
Chase those unbelieving fears;
Look on his deserted grave;
Doubt no more his power to save.

Ye who are of death afraid,
Triumph in the scattered shade;
Drive your anxious cares away;
See the place where Jesus lay!

So the rising sun appears,
Shedding radiance o'er the spheres;
So returning beams of light
Chase the terrors of the night.

Songs for Home-Worship.

HOLLEY. 7s.
GEORGE HEWS.

181.
What though downy slumbers flee,
Strangers to my couch and me?
Sleepless, well I know to rest,
Lodged within my Father's breast.

While the stars unnumbered roll
Round the ever-constant pole,
Far above these spangled skies
All my soul to God shall rise,

'Mid the silence of the night,
Mingling with those angels bright,
Whose harmonious voices raise
Ceaseless love and ceaseless praise.

Through the throng his gentle ear
Shall my tuneless accents hear;
From on high doth he impart
Secret comfort to my heart.

182.
Depth of mercy! — can there be
Mercy still reserved for me?
Can my God his wrath forbear?
Me, the chief of sinners, spare?

I have long withstood his grace,
Long provoked him to his face,
Would not hearken to his calls,
Grieved him by a thousand falls.

There for me the Saviour stands,
Shows his wounds, and spreads his hands:
God is love! I know, I feel;
Jesus weeps, but loves me still.

Now incline me to repent;
Let me now my sins lament,
Now my foul revolt deplore,
Weep, believe, and sin no more.

STEELE. L. M.
Tenderly.
HASTINGS.

183.
My dear Redeemer and my Lord,
I read my duty in thy Word;
But in thy life the law appears,
Drawn out in living characters.

Such was thy truth, and such thy zeal,
Such deference to thy Father's will,
Such love, and meekness so divine,
I would transcribe and make them mine.

Cold mountains and the midnight air
Witnessed the fervor of thy prayer;
The desert thy temptations knew,
Thy conflict, and thy victory too.

Be thou my pattern; make me bear
More of thy gracious image here:
Then God, the Judge, shall own my name
Amongst the followers of the Lamb.

184.
O Lord! how full of sweet content
Our years of pilgrimage are spent!
Where'er we dwell, we dwell with thee, —
In heaven, in earth, or on the sea.

To us remains nor place nor time;
Our country is in every clime:
We can be calm and free from care
On any shore, since God is there.

While place we seek, or place we shun,
The soul finds happiness in none;
But, with our God to guide our way,
'Tis equal joy to go or stay.

Could we be cast where thou art not,
That were indeed a dreadful lot;
But regions none remote we call,
Secure of finding God in all.

Songs for Home-Worship.

STONEFIELD. L. M.   STANLEY.

185. Through every age, eternal God,
Thou art our rest, our safe abode;
High was thy throne ere heaven was made,
Or earth thy humble footstool laid.

Long hadst thou reigned ere time began,
Or dust was fashioned into man;
And long thy kingdom shall endure
When earth and time shall be no more.

Death, like an overflowing stream,
Sweeps us away: our life's a dream;
An empty tale; a morning flower,
Cut down and withered in an hour.

Teach us, O Lord! how frail is man,
And kindly lengthen out our span,
Till a wise care of piety
Fit us to die, and dwell with thee.

186. Great God, whose universal sway
The known and unknown worlds obey,
Now give the kingdom to thy Son,
Extend his power, exalt his throne.

As rain on meadows newly mown,
So shall he send his influence down;
His grace on fainting souls distils
Like heavenly dew on thirsty hills.

The heathen lands, that lie beneath
The shade of overspreading death,
Revive at his first dawning light,
And deserts blossom at the sight.

The saints shall flourish in his days,
Dressed in the robes of joy and praise;
Peace, like a river, from his throne
Shall flow to nations yet unknown.

HORTON. 7s.   WARTENSEE.

187. "Come," said Jesus' sacred voice,—
"Come, and make my paths your choice;
I will guide you to your home :
Weary pilgrim, hither come!

"Thou who, houseless, sole, forlorn,
Long hast borne the proud world's scorn,
Long hast roamed the barren waste,
Weary pilgrim, hither haste!

"Ye who, tossed on beds of pain,
Seek for ease, but seek in vain;
Ye by fiercer anguish torn,
In remorse for guilt who mourn,—

"Hither come! for here is found
Balm that flows for every wound;
Peace that ever shall endure;
Rest eternal, sacred, sure."

188. Lord, we come before thee now;
At thy feet we humbly bow.
Oh! do not our suit disdain:
Shall we seek thee, Lord, in vain?

Lord, on thee our souls depend:
In compassion now descend,
Fill our hearts with thy rich grace,
Tune our lips to sing thy praise.

Comfort those who weep and mourn;
Let the time of joy return;
Those who are cast down, lift up,
Strong in faith, in love, and hope.

Grant that all may seek and find
Thee a God supremely kind;
Heal the sick, the captive free;
Let us all rejoice in thee.

Songs for Home-Worship.

NUREMBERG. 7s.

189.
Thine forever! Lord of life,
Shield us through our earthly strife;
Thou, the Life, the Truth, the Way,
Guide us to the realms of day.

Thine forever! Oh, how blest
They who find in thee their rest!
Saviour, Guardian, heavenly Friend,
Oh! defend us to the end.

Thine forever! Saviour, keep
These thy frail and trembling sheep:
Safe alone beneath thy care,
Let us all thy goodness share.

Thine forever! — thou our Guide,
All our wants by thee supplied,
All our sins by thee forgiven,
Led by thee from earth to heaven.

190.
Glory to the Father give, —
God, in whom we move and live:
Children's songs delight his ear;
Children's prayers he deigns to hear.

Glory to the Son we bring, —
Christ, our Prophet, Priest, and King:
Children, raise your sweetest strain
To the Lamb; for he was slain.

Glory to the Holy Ghost:
He reclaims the sinner lost:
Children's minds may he inspire,
Touch their tongues with holy fire!

Glory in the highest be
To the blessed Trinity,
For the gospel from above,
For the word that "God is love."

OLD HUNDRED. L. M.

191.
Arm of the Lord, awake, awake!
Put on thy strength: the nations shake;
And let the world, adoring, see
Triumphs of mercy wrought by thee.

Say to the heathen from thy throne,
"I am Jehovah, God alone:"
Thy voice their idols shall confound,
And cast their altars to the ground.

No more let human blood be spilt,
Vain sacrifice for human guilt;
But to each conscience be applied
The blood that flowed from Jesus' side.

Almighty God, thy grace proclaim;
In every land declare thy name:
Let adverse powers before thee fall,
And crown the Saviour Lord of all.

192.
New every morning is the love
Our wakening and uprising prove;
Through sleep and darkness safely brought,
Restored to life and power and thought.

New mercies, each returning day,
Hover around us when we pray;
New perils past, new sins forgiven,
New thoughts of God, new hopes of heaven.

If on our daily course our mind
Be set to hallow all we find,
New treasures still, of countless price,
God will provide for sacrifice.

Old friends, old scenes, will lovelier be
As more of heaven in each we see:
Some softening gleam of love and prayer
Shall dawn on every cross and care.

Songs for Home-Worship.

SOLNEY. 8s and 7s.

193.
Tarry with me, O my Saviour;
For the day is passing by:
See! the shades of evening gather,
And the night is drawing nigh.

Deeper, deeper, grow the shadows;
Paler now the glowing west:
Swift the night of death advances;
Shall it be the night of rest?

Feeble, trembling, fainting, dying,
Lord, I cast myself on thee:
Tarry with me through the darkness;
While I sleep, still watch by me.

Tarry with me, O my Saviour!
Lay my head upon thy breast
Till the morning; then awake me,—
Morning of eternal rest!

194.
Gently, Lord, oh! gently lead us
Through this lonely vale of tears,
Through the changes thou'st decreed us,
Till our last great change appears.

When temptation's darts assail us,
When in devious paths we stray,
Let thy goodness never fail us;
Lead us in thy perfect way.

In the hour of pain and anguish,
In the hour when death draws near,
Suffer not our hearts to languish,
Suffer not our souls to fear.

And, when mortal life is ended,
Bid us on thy bosom rest,
Till, by angel-bands attended,
We awake among the blest.

Spirited.

MENDON. L. M.

195.
A little child the Saviour came;
The mighty God was still his name:
And angels worshipped as he lay,
The seeming infant of a day.

He who, a little child, began
The life divine to show to man,
Proclaims from heaven the message free,—
"Let little children come to Me."

We bring them, Lord, and, with the sign
Of Holy Spirit, name them thine;
Their souls with saving grace endow;
Baptize them with thy Spirit now.

Oh! give thine angels charge, good Lord,
Them safely in thy way to guard;
Thy blessings on their lives command,
And write their names upon thy hand.

196.
No change of time shall ever shock
My firm affection, Lord, to thee;
For thou hast always been my rock,
A fortress and defence to me.

To thee I will address my prayer,
To whom all praise we justly owe;
So shall I, by thy watchful care,
Be guarded safe from every foe.

Let the eternal Lord be praised,—
The Rock on whose defence I rest;
To highest heavens His name be raised
Who me with his salvation blest.

My God, to celebrate thy fame,
My grateful voice to heaven I'll raise;
And nations, strangers to thy name,
Shall learn to sing thy glorious praise.

Songs for Home-Worship.

AMERICA. National Hymn. 6s & 4s.

197.

My country, 'tis of thee,
Sweet land of liberty,
Of thee I sing:
Land where my fathers died,
Land of the pilgrims' pride,
From every mountain-side
Let freedom ring.

My native country, thee,
Land of the noble free,
Thy name I love;
I love thy rocks and rills,
Thy woods and templed hills;
My heart with rapture thrills
Like that above.

Let music swell the breeze,
And ring from all the trees
Sweet Freedom's song;
Let mortal tongues awake;
Let all that breathe partake;
Let rocks their silence break,
The sound prolong.

Our fathers' God, to thee,
Author of liberty,
To thee we sing:
Long may our land be bright
With freedom's holy light!
Protect us by thy might,
Great God, our King.

SWEET HOUR OF PRAYER. Wm. B. Bradbury.

198.

Sweet hour of prayer!
That calls me from a world of care,
And bids me at my Father's throne
Make all my wants and wishes known.
In seasons of distress and grief,
My soul has often found relief,
And oft escaped the tempter's snare,
By thy return, sweet hour of prayer!

Sweet hour of prayer!
Thy wings shall my petition bear
To Him whose truth and faithfulness
Engage the waiting soul to bless;
And since he bids me seek his face,
Believe his word, and trust his grace,
I'll cast on him my every care,
And wait for thee, sweet hour of prayer!

Sweet hour of prayer!
May I thy consolation share,
Till from Mount Pisgah's lofty height
I view my home, and take my flight!
This robe of flesh I'll drop, and rise
To seize the everlasting prize;
And shout, while passing through the air,
"Farewell, farewell, sweet hour of prayer!"

ROCK OF AGES. 7s. Dr. T. Hastings.

199.

Rock of ages, cleft for me,
Let me hide myself in thee;
Let the water and the blood
From thy wounded side that flowed
Be of sin the perfect cure;
Save me, Lord, and make me pure.

Should my tears forever flow,
Should my zeal no languor know,
This for sin could ne'er atone:
Thou must save, and thou alone.
In my hand no price I bring;
Simply to thy cross I cling.

While I draw this fleeting breath,
When mine eyelids close in death,
When I rise to worlds unknown,
And behold thee on thy throne,
Rock of ages, cleft for me,
Let me hide myself in thee.

Songs for Home-Worship.

Words by (V.)   **WELCOME HOUR OF PRAYER.**   WM. B. BRADBURY.

200.

When softly o'er the distant hills
The beams of morning break,
When Nature breathes her choral hymn,
My cheerful heart shall wake;
My strength renewed, my soul refreshed,
I'll bless a Father's care,
And hail with pure and holy joy
The welcome hour of prayer.

When, like a giant in his course,
The glorious orb of light,
Ascending in the radiant sky,
Has reached his noonday height,
From earthly scenes I'll turn away
To bless a Father's care,
And hail with pure and holy joy
The welcome hour of prayer.

When slowly fades the silent eve
Beneath the glowing west,
And tranquil thoughts of heavenly peace
Within my bosom rest,
For all the mercies of the day
I'll bless a Father's care,
And hail with pure and holy joy
The welcome hour of prayer.

Allegro.   **ITALIAN HYMN. 6s and 4s.**   GIARDINI.

201.

Come, thou Almighty King!
Help us thy name to sing;
Help us to praise:
Father all-glorious,
O'er all victorious,
Come and reign over us,
Ancient of days.

Jesus, our Lord, arise;
Scatter our enemies;
Now make them fall:
Let thine almighty aid
Our sure defence be made,
Our souls on thee be stayed;
Lord, hear our call.

Come, thou incarnate Word,
Gird on thy mighty sword;
Our prayer attend:
Come, and thy people bless;
Come, give thy word success;
Spirit of holiness,
On us descend.

CHRISTMAS. C. M. Double.

202.

While shepherds watched their flocks by night,
All seated on the ground,
An angel of the Lord came down,
And glory shone around.

"Fear not," said he (for mighty dread
Had seized their troubled mind);
"Glad tidings of great joy I bring
To you and all mankind.

"To you, in David's town, this day,
Is born of David's line
The Saviour, who is Christ, the Lord;
And this shall be the sign:—

"The heavenly Babe you there shall find
To human view displayed,
All meanly wrapped in swathing-bands,
And in a manger laid."

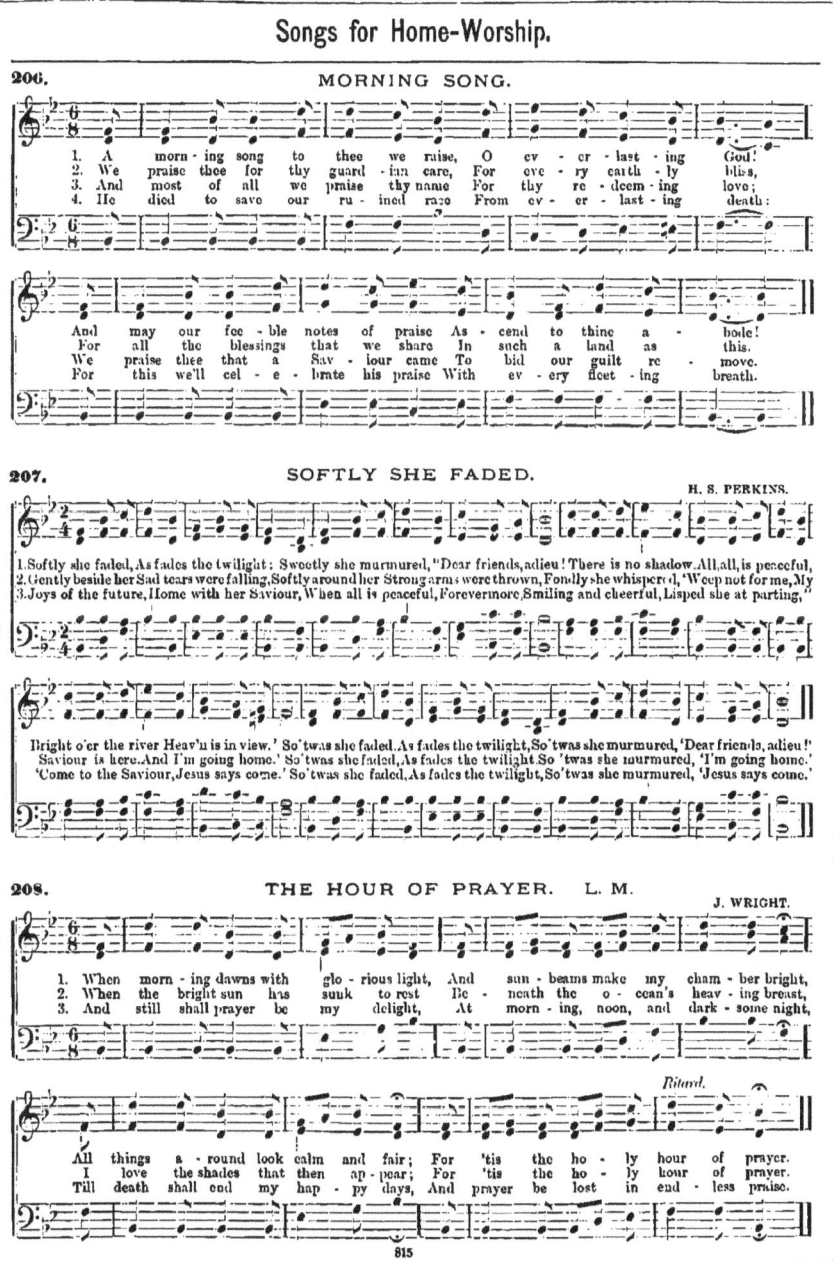

Songs for Home-Worship.

211. PRAISE THE GIVER OF ALL.
SUITABLE FOR A FESTIVAL.
WM. F. SHERWIN.

1. Let us mingle our voices in chorus to-day; The earth is rejoicing, all nature is gay,
2. There is joy in the sunbeam that sparkles so bright, And calls the young blossoms to welcome the light;
3. Let us join the glad music, and joyfully raise, In purest devotion, our jubilant praise;

And the stream in the valley goes laughing along; How happy its beautiful song!
D.C. Let his children with rapture his mercy recall, The bountiful Giver of all;
And the bird in the greenwood is singing with glee, As cheerful and happy as we.
We are grateful to God for this beautiful day, We'll sing the bright moments away.

CHORUS.
Praise the Lord, the Giver of all; Praise the Lord, the Giver of all.

212. DEAR JESUS. 8s & 6s.
AUGUSTE MIGNON.

1. Dear Jesus! ever at my side, How loving must thou be To leave thy home in
2. I cannot feel thee touch my hand With pressure light and mild, To check me as my
3. And when, dear Saviour! I kneel down, Morning and night, to prayer, Something there is with-

heaven to guard A little child like me! Thy beautiful and shining face I
mother did When I was but a child. But I have felt thee in my thoughts Fight-
in my heart Which tells me thou art there. Yes, when I pray, thou pray'rest too; Thy

see not, tho' so near; The sweetness of thy soft, low voice, I am too deaf to hear.
ing with sin for me; And, when my heart loves God, I know The sweetness is from thee.
prayer is all for me: But when I sleep, thou sleepest not, But watchest patiently.

Songs for Home-Worship.

213. NATIONAL. *Words and Music by Dr. HASTINGS.*

Quick and joyous.

1. How swiftly the years have been rolling away! And many have rapidly sped Since first the bright Union we cherish to-day Its banners to enterprise led.
2. Tho' few now remain who were early employed In founding the fabric we love, Full many its blessings have richly enjoyed, And gone to their mansions above.
3. Let teachers with parents and children unite In songs of thanksgiving and praise; Recounting God's blessing with holy delight, Adoring his works and his ways.
4. And may the rich dews of the Spirit distil, Our prayers and our labors to own, Till converts unnumbered our temples shall fill, The Prince of salvation to crown.

CHORUS.

Our Union forever! 'tis bound to prevail, While multitudes joyful its jubilee hail.

214. OUR HEARTS ARE YOUNG AND JOYOUS. *WM. B. BRADBURY.*

1. Our hearts are young and joyous; 'Tis spring-time with us now: The dew of life's bright morning Is fresh upon each brow. The world to us seems pleasant, With love its joys to share. God, in his tender kindness, Hath made it very fair.
2. Oh! can we e'er forget Him Who is so good and kind? No: rather would we love him With all our heart and mind. But we can never Oh! help us then, dear Saviour, To til our hearts are clean: The precious blood of Jesus Must wash them first from sin.
3. We know the harps of heaven Would sound a gladder strain, "There's joy among the angels," When one repents of sin. Oh! help us then, dear Saviour, To give our hearts to thee: Let us, in youth's glad morning, Thy loved disciples be.
4. And when upon our foreheads The silver locks shall fall, Or early comes the shadow, Which comes alike to all; Still safe upon thy bosom Our spirits shall recline, And, 'mid the joys of heaven, We shall be ever thine.

Songs for Home-Worship.

215.   SUNDAY-SCHOOL VOLUNTEER SONG.

To the Leader.—The effect of this piece will be heightened by singing the first part responsively.

Words written for this work.   WM. B. BRADBURY.
In marching movement.

1. We are marching on with shield and banner bright; We will work for God, and battle for the right; We will
  In the Sunday school our ar-my we prepare, As we ral-ly round our blessed standard there, And the
D.C. We are marching onward, singing as we go, To the promised land, where living waters flow; Come and

2. We are marching on: our Captain, ev-er near, Will protect us still; His gen-tle voice we hear: Let the
  Then awake, a-wake, our happy, happy song, We will shout for joy, and glad-ly march along; In the

3. We are marching on the strait and narrow way That will lead to life and ev-er-last-ing day, To the
  We are marching on and pressing toward the prize, To a glorious crown beyond the glowing skies, To the

praise his name, rejoicing in his might, And we'll work till Je-sus calls. } Then awake, Then a-wake, hap-py
Saviour's cross we early learn to bear, While we work till Jo - sus calls.
join our ranks as pilgrims here below, Come and work till Je-sus calls.
foe advance, we'll never, ne-ver fear, For we'll work till Je - sus calls.
Lord of hosts let every heart be strong, While we'll work till Je-sus calls.
smiling fields that never will decay; But we'll work till Je-sus calls.
radiant fields where pleasure never dies, And we'll work till Jesus calls.

Then awake,   Then awake,   D.C.

song.   happy song,   Shout for joy,   shout for joy,   As we glad - ly march a - long,   D.C.

happy song,...... happy song,   Shout for joy,   shout for joy, As we glad-ly march a - long.

216.   THE SAVIOUR'S LOVE.

DUET. *Moderato.*   LESTA VESE.

1. Soft be the gen - tle breathing notes That sing the Saviour's dy - ing love;
2. Soft as the morn - ing dews de - scend, While the sweet lark ex - ult - ing soars,
3. Pure as the stars' en - liven - ing ray, That scatters life and joy a - broad;
4. Pure as the breath of ver - nal skies, So pure let our con - tri - tion be;

Soft as the eve - ning ze - phyr floats;   Soft as the tune - ful lyres a - bove.
So soft to your Al - migh - ty Friend   Be eve - ry sigh your bo - som pours.
Pure as the glo - rious orb of day,   That wide proclaims its Ma - ker, God.
And pure - ly let our sor - rows rise   To Him who bled up - on the tree.

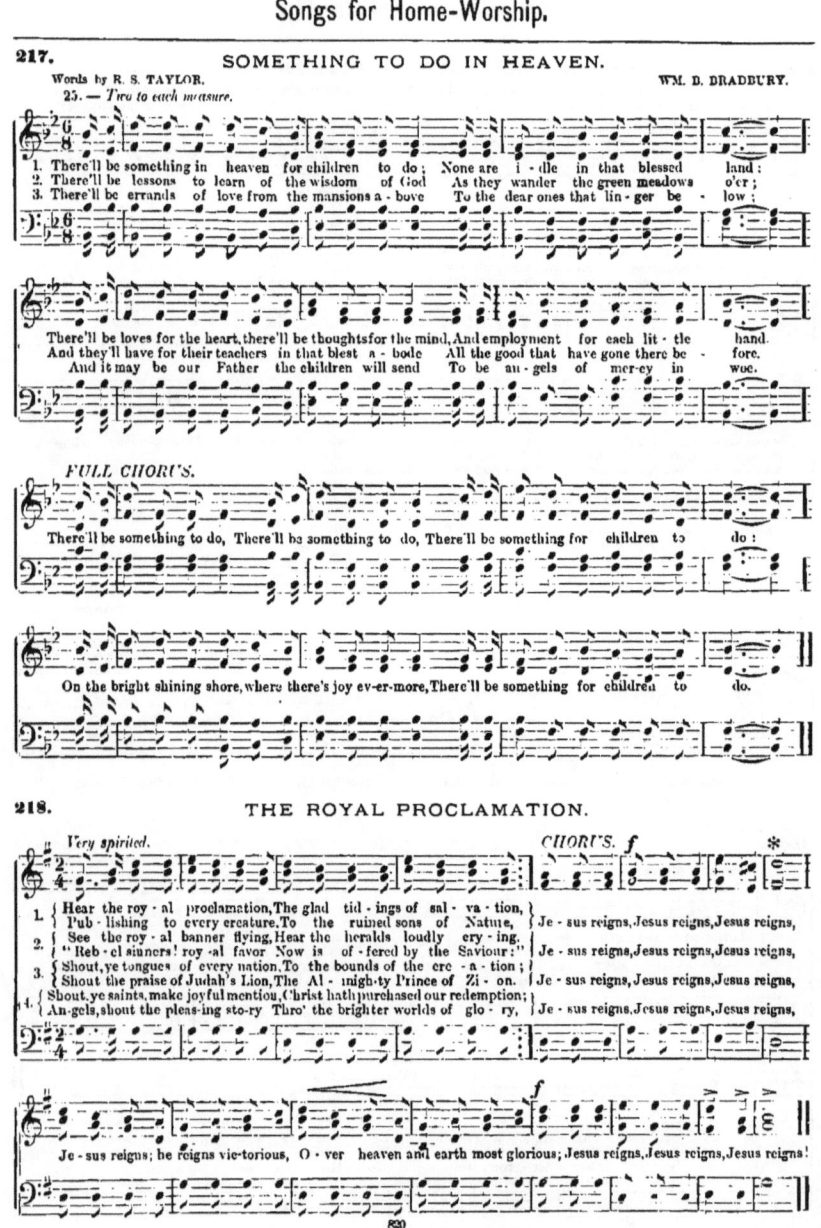

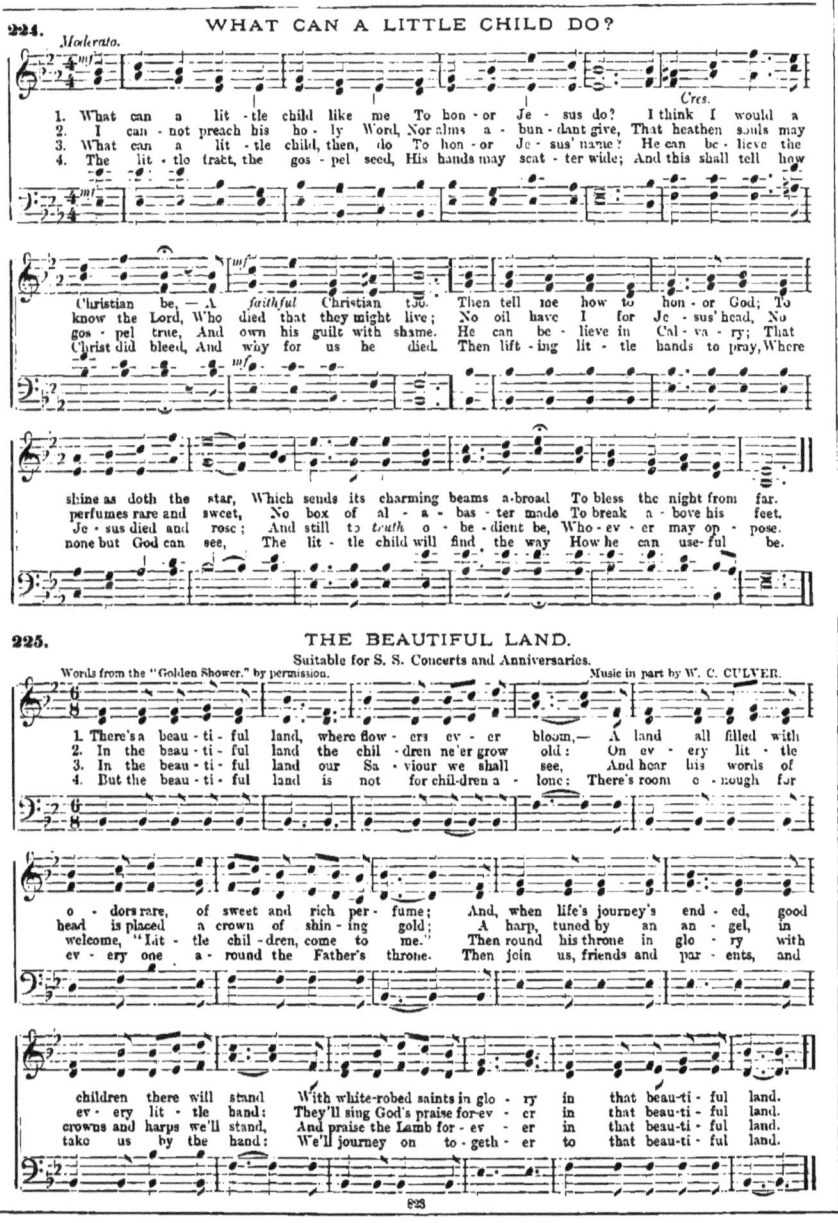

Songs for Home-Worship.

228. THE HEAVENLY LAND.

"A better country; that is, a heavenly." — *Heb.* xi. 16.

1. I love to think of the heavenly land, Where white-robed angels are; Where
2. I love to think of the heavenly land, Where my Redeemer reigns; Where
3. I love to think of the heavenly land, The saints' eternal home; Where
4. I love to think of the heavenly land; The greetings there we'll meet; The
5. I love to think of the heavenly land, That promised land so fair. Oh,

many a friend is gathered safe From fear and toil and care. There'll be no
rapturous songs of triumph rise In endless, joyous strains. There'll be no
palms and robes and crowns ne'er fade, And all our joys are one. There'll be no
harps, the songs, for ever ours; The walks, the golden streets. There'll be no
how my raptured spirit longs To be forever there! There'll be no

part-ing, There'll be no part-ing, There'll be no part-ing, There'll be no part-ing there.

229. "WE LIFT OUR TUNEFUL VOICES." (Picnic Song.)

KARL REDEN.

mf Cheerfully.

1. { We lift our tuneful voices now In fresh melodious song, } And, as we send our
   { While youthful eyes with pleasure glow To see our happy throng. }
2. { And ye who join the swelling lay, Sweet melodies employ, } Our teachers kind, whose
   { To cheer us on our upward way, And praises blend with joy. }

greeting to The breezes soft and mild, Let waves of cheerful praises flow From pure hearts undefiled.
constant care We honor and approve, Let smiles, which all our faces wear, Reward your works of love.

f CHORUS. *cres.* *Repeat.* **pp**

Tra, la, tra, la, la, la, tra, la, tra, la, la, la, tra, la, la, la, la, la, la, la, tra, la, la, la, la.

Songs for Home-Worship.

230. GENTLE WORDS.
Not too fast.   LESTA VESE.

1. The sun may warm the grass to life, The dew the droop-ing flower;
2. But words that breathe of ten - der - ness, And smiles we know are true,
3. They fall like gen - tle sum-mer - rain On parched and thirs - ty ground.
4. Bright smiles are like the morn - ing sun Shin - ing with ra - diant light:

The eyes grow bright, and watch the light Of Au - tumn's o - pening hour:
Are warm - er than the sum - mer - time, And bright - er than the dew.
Such words none ev - er speak in vain: How sweet their thrill-ing sound!
Kind words, when heard from an - y one, Will make some life more bright.

231. THE BEAUTIFUL WAY.
FANNY.   CHESTER G. ALLEN.

1. Beau - ti - ful way, hallowed and blest, Lead - ing us home to a man - sion of rest:
2. Soft - ly a voice mur - murs with - in, "Turn from the world and the pleas - ures of sin;
3. Beau - ti - ful way, peace - ful and bright, Gent - ly from E - den re - flect - ing its light;
4. Beau - ti - ful way, glad - ly we sing; Praise and thanksgiv - ing to Je - sus we bring:

Wis - dom de - clares, "Hap - py are they, Walk - ing with God in the beau - ti - ful way."
Come and re - joice; why will ye stay? Walk in the shin - ing, the beau - ti - ful way.
Cheer-ful the beam, tran - quil the ray, Guid - ing the soul in the beau - ti - ful way.
Still may his love teach us to pray, Help us to walk in the beau - ti - ful way!

232. MORNING WALKS.
                         SWEDISH MELODY.

1. { A - wake from your slum - ber, and come with a song } The birds sing to
    { Through mead-ows and for - ests and wood - lands a - long;
2. { The wood - lands are filled with sweet breath from the sky; } The town at our
    { Our step is un - tir - ing, our spir - its are high.
3. { Leap o - ver the chasms, with wings to our feet; } No oak of the
    { Climb up to the tree - tops, the heav - ens to greet.

wel - come the morn - ing and you, And sip their first break - fast of new - fall - en dew.
backs, and the moun - tains in view, What joy is a - wait - ing your com - rades and you!
for - est for us is too high: The far - ther from earth we are, near - er the sky.

Songs for Home-Worship.

233.

SING HALLELUJAH.

Words from the "Polyphonic," by permission.

1. We are on the o-cean sail-ing; Homeward bound we sweet-ly glide; We are on the o-cean,
2. Come on board; oh! ship for glo-ry; Be in haste; make up your mind: For our vessel's weighing
3. You have kindred o-ver yon-der, On that bright and happy shore: By and by we'll swell the
4. When we all are safe-ly land-ed, We will shout our tri-als o'er; We will walk a-bout the

CHORUS.

sail-ing To a home beyond the tide. All the storms will soon be over; Then we'll anchor safe in harbor. We are
anchor; You will soon be left behind. All the storms will soon be over, Then we'll anchor safe in harbor. We are
number,When the toils of life are o'er. All the storms will soon be over,Then we'll anchor safe in harbor. We are
ci-ty, And we'll sing forev-er more. All the storms of life are o-ver, Landed in a port of glo-ry; No more

With spirit.

on the ocean, sailing To a home beyond the tide, Where we'll sing halle-lu-jah, sing hal-le-lu-jah,
Last verse.
on the ocean sailing, Safe at home beyond the tide. And we'll sing halle-lu-jah, sing hal-le-lu-jah,

Sing halle-lu-jah to God and the Lamb,Sing halle-lu-jah, sing hal-le-lujah,Sing hallelujah to God and the Lamb!

234.

THE GRACIOUS CHOICE.

E. ROBERTS.

1. Come, children, join to sing, Hal-le-lu-jah! A-men! Loud praise to Christ our King, Hallelujah! A-
2. Come, lift your hearts on high, Hal-le-lu-jah! A-men! Let praises fill the sky, Hal-le-lu-jah! A-
3. Praise yet the Lord a-gain, Hal-le-lu-jah! A-men! Life shall not end the strain, Halle-lu-jah! A-

men! Let all with heart and voice Before his throne rejoice; Praise is his gracious choice, Hallelujah! A-men.
men! He is our guide and friend; To us he'll con-descend; His love shall never end,Hal-le-lu-jah! A-men.
men! On heaven's blissful shore His goodness we'll adore; Singing forev-er more, Hal-le-lu-jah! A-men.

Songs for Home-Worship.

235. HEBER. C. M.

John Newton. G. Kingsley.

1 How sweet the Name of Jesus sounds
  In a believer's ear;
 It soothes his sorrows, heals his wounds,
  And drives away his fear.

2 It makes the wounded spirit whole,
  And calms the troubled breast;
 'Tis manna to the hungry soul,
  And, to the weary, rest.

3 Jesus, my Shepherd, Brother, Friend,
  My Prophet, Priest, and King;

My Lord, my Life, my Way, my End,
  Accept the praise I bring.

4 Weak is the effort of my heart,
  And cold my warmest thought;
 But when I see Thee as Thou art,
  I'll praise Thee as I ought.

5 Till then I would Thy love proclaim
  With every fleeting breath;
 And may the music of Thy Name
  Refresh my soul in death.

236. THE SWEETEST NAME.

Rev. Geo. W. Bethune, D. D., 1858. Wm. B. Bradbury.

1 There is no name so sweet on earth,
  No name so sweet in heaven,
 The name before his wondrous birth
  To Christ, the Saviour given.

Cho.—We love to sing around our king,
  And hail him blessed Jesus;
 For there's no word ear ever heard,
  So dear, so sweet, as Jesus.

2 His human name they did proclaim,
  When Abram's son they seal'd him;

The name that still by God's good will,
  Deliverer revealed him.—Cho.

3 And when he hung upon the tree,
  They wrote his name above him,
 That all might see the reason we
  For evermore must love him.—Cho.

4 So now upon his Father's throne,
  Almighty to release us
 From sin and pains, he gladly reigns,
  The Prince and Saviour, Jesus.—Cho.

Copyright, 1861, by Wm. B. Bradbury. From "Golden Chain," by permission.

237. STEPHANOS. 8.5.8.3.

J. M. Neale. H. W. Baker.

1 Art thou weary, art thou languid?
  Art thou sore distressed?
 "Come to Me," saith One, "and coming,
  Be at rest."

2 Hath He marks to lead me to Him,
  If He be my Guide?
 "In His feet and hands are wound-prints;
  And His side."

3 Is there diadem, as Monarch,
  That His brow adorns?

"Yea, a crown, in very surety,
  But of thorns."

4 If I find Him, if I follow,
  What His guerdon here?
 "Many a sorrow, many a labor,
  Many a tear."

5 If I still hold closely to Him,
  What hath He at last?
 "Sorrow vanquish'd, labor ended,
  Jordan passed."

Songs for Home-Worship.

238. I NEED THEE EVERY HOUR.

Mrs. Annie S. Hawks.   Rev. R. Lowry.

REFRAIN.

1 I need thee every hour,
   Most gracious Lord ;
   No tender voice like thine
   Can peace afford.
   Cho.—I need thee, oh ! I need thee ;
   Every hour I need thee ;
   O bless me now, my Saviour !
   I come to thee.

2 I need thee every hour ;
   Stay thou near by ;
   Temptations lose their pow'r
   When thou art nigh.—*Cho.*

3 I need thee every hour,
   In joy or pain ;
   Come quickly and abide,
   Or life is vain.—*Cho.*

4 I need thee every hour ;
   Teach me thy will ;
   And thy rich promises
   In me fulfill.—*Cho.*

5 I need thee every hour,
   Most Holy One ;
   Oh, make me thine indeed,
   Thou blessed Son.—*Cho.*

Copyright, 1872, by R. Lowry. From "Royal Diadem," by permission Biglow & Main.

Charlotte Elliott.   239. WOODWORTH. L. M.   Wm. B. Bradbury.

1 Just as I am, without one plea,
   But that Thy blood was shed for me,
   And that Thou bid'st me come to Thee,
   O Lamb of God, I come ! I come !

2 Just as I am, and waiting not,
   To rid my soul of one dark blot,
   To Thee, whose blood can cleanse each spot,
   O Lamb of God, I come ! I come !

3 Just as I am, though tossed about
   With many a conflict, many a doubt,

Fightings and fears within, without,
   O Lamb of God, I come ! I come !

4 Just as I am, Thou wilt receive,
   Wilt welcome, pardon, cleanse, relieve ;
   Because Thy promise I believe,
   O Lamb of God, I come ! I come !

5 Just as I am, Thy love unknown
   Has broken every barrier down ;
   Now, to be Thine, yea, Thine alone,
   O Lamb of God, I come ! I come !

Songs for Home-Worship.

240. NEAR THE CROSS.

FANNY J. CROSBY. W. H. DOANE.

1 Jesus, keep me near the Cross,
  There a precious fountain,
  Free to all, a healing stream,
  Flows from Calvary's mountain.

Cho.—In the Cross, in the Cross
  Be my glory ever,
  Till my raptured soul shall find
  Rest beyond the river.

2 Near the Cross, a trembling soul,
  Love and mercy found me;

There the bright and morning star
Shed its beams around me.—*Cho.*

3 Near the Cross! oh, Lamb of God,
  Bring its scenes before me;
  Help me walk from day to day,
  With its shadow o'er me.—*Cho.*

4 Near the Cross I'll watch and wait,
  Hoping, trusting ever,
  Till I reach the golden strand,
  Just beyond the river.—*Cho.*

Copyright, 1869, by BIGLOW & MAIN. From "BRIGHT JEWELS," by permission.

241. MARTYN. 7. D.

CHARLES WESLEY. S. B. MARSH.

1 Jesus, Lover of my soul,
  Let me to thy bosom fly,
  While the nearer waters roll,
  While the tempest still is high;
  Hide me, O my Saviour, hide,
  Till the storm of life be past;
  Safe into the haven guide;
  O receive my soul at last.

2 Other refuge have I none;
  Hangs my helpless soul on thee;
  Leave, ah! leave me not alone,
  Still support and comfort me!
  All my trust on thee is stayed,
  All my help from thee I bring
  Cover my defenceless head
  With the shadow of thy wing.

3 Thou, O Christ, art all I want;
  More than all in thee I find.
  Raise the fallen, cheer the faint,
  Heal the sick, and lead the blind.
  Just and holy is thy name;
  I am all unrighteousness;
  False and full of sin I am,
  Thou art full of truth and grace.

4 Plenteous grace with thee is found,
  Grace to cover all my sin;
  Let the healing streams abound,
  Make and keep me pure within.
  Thou of Life the Fountain art;
  Freely let me take of thee;
  Spring thou up within my heart,
  Rise to all eternity.

Songs for Home-Worship.

242. THE OLD, OLD STORY.

CATHERINE HANKEY. 1867.   W. H. DOANE.

1 Tell me the old, old story
  Of unseen things above,
  Of Jesus and his glory,
  Of Jesus and his love.
  Tell me the story simply,
  As to a little child,
  For I am weak and weary,
  And helpless and defiled.
  Cho.—Tell me the old, old story,
       Tell me the old, old story,
       Tell me the old, old story,
       Of Jesus and his love.

2 Tell me the story slowly,
  That I may take it in—
  That wonderful redemption,
  God's remedy for sin.
  Tell me the story often,
  For I forget so soon!

The "early dew" of morning
Has passed away at noon.—*Cho.*

3 Tell me the story softly,
  With earnest tones, and grave;
  Remember! I'm the sinner
  Whom Jesus came to save.
  Tell me that story always,
  If you would really be
  In any time of trouble,
  A comforter to me.—*Cho.*

4 Tell me the same old story,
  When you have cause to fear
  That this world's empty glory
  Is costing me too dear.
  Yes, and when that world's glory
  Is drawing on my soul,
  Tell me the old, old story:
  "Christ Jesus makes thee whole."—*Cho.*

Copyright, 1870, by W. H. DOANE. From "SONGS OF DEVOTION," by per. BIGLOW & MAIN.

ROBERT ROBINSON.   **243. STOCKWELL. 8.7.8.7.**   D. E. JONES.

1 Saviour, source of every blessing,
  Tune my heart to grateful lays;
  Streams of mercy, never ceasing,
  Call for ceaseless songs of praise.
2 Teach me some melodious measure,
  Sung by raptured saints above;
  Fill my soul with sacred pleasure,
  While I sing redeeming love.

3 Thou didst seek me when a stranger,
  Wandering from the fold of God;
  Thou, to rescue me from danger,
  Didst redeem me with thy blood.
4 By thy hand restored, defended,
  Safe through life thus far I'm come;
  Safe, O Lord, when life is ended,
  Bring me to my heavenly home.

Songs for Home-Worship.

FANNY J. CROSBY. **244. EVERY DAY AND HOUR.** **W. H. DOANE.**

1 Saviour, more than life to me,
I am clinging, clinging close to thee;
Let thy precious blood applied,
Keep me ever, ever near thy side.

Ref.—Every day (and hour), every day (and hour),
Let me feel thy cleansing, cleansing power;
May thy tender love to me
Bind me closer, closer, Lord, to thee.

2 Through this changing world below,
Lead me gently, gently as I go;
Trusting thee, I cannot stray,
I can never, never lose my way.—*Ref.*

3 Let me love thee more and more,
Till this fleeting, fleeting life is o'er;
Till my soul is lost in love,
In a brighter, brighter world above.—*Ref.*

Copyright, 1875, by BIGLOW & MAIN. From "BRIGHTEST AND BEST," by permission.

RAY PALMER. **245. OLIVET. 6.4.** **L. MASON.**

1 My faith looks up to thee,
Thou Lamb of Calvary,
Saviour divine!
Now hear me while I pray;
Take all my guilt away;
O let me from this day,
Be wholly thine.

2 May thy rich grace impart
Strength to my fainting heart;
My zeal inspire;
As thou hast died for me,
O may my love to thee
Pure, warm, and changeless be,
A living fire.

3 While life's dark maze I tread,
And griefs around me spread,
Be thou my guide;
Bid darkness turn to day,
Wipe sorrow's tears away,
Nor let me ever stray
From thee aside.

4 When ends life's transient dream,
When death's cold, sullen stream
Shall o'er me roll,
Blest Saviour, then, in love,
Fear and distress remove;
O bear me safe above,
A ransomed soul.

Songs for Home-Worship.

246. PORTUGUESE HYMN.

GEORGE KEITH. J. READING.

1 How firm a foundation, ye saints of the Lord,
Is laid for your faith in his excellent word;
What more can he say than to you he hath said,
Who unto the Saviour for refuge have fled.

2 "Fear not, I am with thee, O be not dismayed,
For I am thy God, and will still give thee aid;
I'll strengthen thee, aid thee, and cause thee to
Upheld by my righteous, omnipotent hand. [stand,

3 "When thro' the deep waters I call thee to go,
The rivers of sorrow shall not overflow;
For I will be with thee thy trouble to bless,
And sanctify to thee thy deepest distress.

4 "The soul that on Jesus hath leaned for repose
I will not, I will not desert to his foes;
That soul, tho' all hell should endeavor to shake,
I'll never, no never, no never forsake."

247. SOMETHING FOR JESUS.

Rev. S. D. PHELPS, D.D. Rev. ROBERT LOWRY.

1 Saviour! thy dying love
Thou gavest me,
Nor should I aught withhold,
Dear Lord, from thee:
In love my soul would bow,
My heart fulfill its vow,
Some off'ring bring thee now,
Something for thee.

2 At the blest mercy-seat,
Pleading for me,
My feeble faith looks up,

Jesus, to thee:
Help me the cross to bear,
Thy wondrous love declare,
Some song to raise, or prayer,
Something for thee.

3 Give me a faithful heart—
Likeness to thee—
That each departing day
Henceforth may see
Some work of love begun,
Some deed of kindness done,

Some wanderer sought and won,
Something for thee.

4 All that I am and have—
Thy gifts so free—
In joy, in grief, through life,
Dear Lord, for thee!
And when thy face I see,
My ransomed soul shall be,
Through all eternity,
Something for thee.

Copyright, 1871. by BIGLOW & MAIN. From "PURE GOLD," by permission.

Songs for Home-Worship.

248. BEAUTIFUL VALLEY OF EDEN.

1 Beautiful valley of Eden!
 Sweet is thy noontide calm;
 Over the hearts of the weary,
 Breathing thy waves of balm.

Cho.—Beautiful valley of Eden,
 Home of the pure and the blest,
 How often amid the wild billows
 I dream of thy rest—sweet rest!

2 Over the heart of the mourner
 Shineth thy golden day,
 Wafting the songs of the angels
 Down from the far away.—Cho.

3 There is the home of my Saviour;
 There, with the blood-wash'd throng,
 Over the highlands of glory
 Rolleth the great, new song.

Copyright, 1877, by Biglow & Main. From "Welcome Tidings," by permission.

249. RETREAT. L. M.

Hugh Stowell. / T. Hastings.

1 From every stormy wind that blows,
 From every swelling tide of woes,
 There is a calm, a sure retreat,
 'Tis found beneath the mercy-seat.

2 There is a place where Jesus sheds
 The oil of gladness on our heads;
 A place than all besides more sweet,
 It is the blood-bought mercy-seat.

3 There is a spot where spirits blend,
 Where friend holds fellowship with friend,
 Tho' sundered far, by faith they meet
 Around the common mercy-seat.

4 There, there on eagle's wings we soar,
 And time and sense seem all no more;
 And heaven comes down our souls to greet,
 And glory crowns the mercy-seat.

5 O, may my hand forget her skill,
 My tongue be silent, cold, and still,
 This bounding heart forget to beat,
 If I forget the mercy-seat.

Songs for Home-Worship.

250. HE LEADETH ME.

Prof. JOS. H. GILMORE.   WM. B. BRADBURY.

1 He leadeth me! oh blessed thought,
  Oh! words with heavenly comfort fraught;
  Whate'er I do, where'er I be,
  Still 'tis God's hand that leadeth me.

Ref.—He leadeth me! He leadeth me!
  By his own hand he leadeth me;
  His faithful follo'wer I would be,
  For by his hand he leadeth me.

2 Sometimes 'mid scenes of deepest gloom,
  Sometimes where Eden's bowers bloom,
  By waters still, o'er troubled sea,—
  Still 'tis his hand that leadeth me.—*Ref.*

3 Lord, I would clasp thy hand in mine,
  Nor ever murmur nor repine—
  Content, whatever lot I see,
  Since 'tis my God that leadeth me.—*Ref.*

4 And when my task on earth is done,
  When, by thy grace, the victory's won,
  E'en death's cold wave I will not flee,
  Since God through Jordan leadeth me.—*Ref.*

Copyright, 1884, by WM. B. BRADBURY. From "GOLDEN CENSER," by per. BIGLOW & MAIN.

251. WOODSTOCK. C. M.

D. DUTTON.

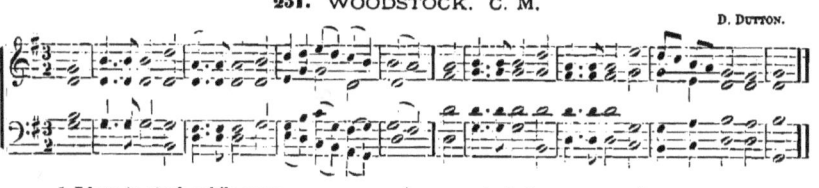

1 I love to steal awhile away
  From every cumbering care,
  And spend the hours of setting day
  In humble, grateful prayer.

2 I love in solitude to shed
  The penitential tear,
  And all his promises to plead,
  Where none but God can hear.

3 I love to think on mercies past,
  And future good implore,
  And all my cares and sorrows cast
  On him whom I adore.

4 I love by faith to take a view
  Of brighter scenes in heaven;
  The prospect doth my strength renew,
  While here by tempests driven.

5 Thus, when life's toilsome day is o'er,
  May its departing ray
  Be calm as this impressive hour,
  And lead to endless day.

Songs for Home-Worship.

252. BLESSED HOME-LAND.

FANNY J. CROSBY.   HUBERT P. MAIN.

1 Gliding o'er life's fitful waters,
   Heavy surges sometimes roll;
   And we sigh for yonder haven,
   For the Homeland of the soul.
Ref.—Blessed Homeland, ever fair!
   Sin can never enter there;
   But the soul, to life awaking,
   Everlasting bloom shall wear.

2 Oft we catch a faint reflection
   Of its bright and vernal hills;
   And, though distant, how we hail it!
   How each heart with rapture thrills!—Ref.

3 To our Father, and our Saviour,
   To the Spirit, three in one,
   We shall sing glad songs of triumph
   When our harvest work is done.—Ref.

4 'Tis the weary pilgrim's Home-land,
   Where each throbbing care shall cease,
   And our longings and our yearnings,
   Like a wave, be hushed to peace.—Ref.

Copyright, 1877, by BIGLOW & MAIN. From "WELCOME TIDINGS," by permission.

253. FREDERICK. II.

WM. A. MUHLENBERG.   G. KINSLEY.

1 I would not live alway; I ask not to stay
   Where storm after storm rises dark o'er the way;
   The few lurid mornings, that dawn on us here,
   Are enough for life's woes, full enough for its cheer.

2 I would not live alway, thus fettered by sin,
   Temptation without and corruption within;
   E'en the rapture of pardon is mingled with fears,
   And the cup of thanksgiving with penitent tears.

3 Who, who would live alway, away from his God;
   Away from yon heaven, that blissful abode,
   Where the rivers of pleasure flow o'er the bright
   And the noontide of glory eternally reigns? [plains,

4 Where the saints of all ages in harmony meet,
   Their Saviour and brethren transported to greet;
   While the anthems of rapture unceasingly roll,
   And the smile of the Lord is the feast of the soul.

Songs for Home-Worship.

254. PASS ME NOT.

FANNY J. CROSBY.   W. H. DOANE.

1 Pass me not, O gentle Saviour,
  Hear my humble cry ;
  While on others thou art smiling,
  Do not pass me by.

Chorus.
Saviour, Saviour, hear my humble cry,
While on others thou art calling,
Do not pass me by.

2 Let me at a throne of mercy
  Find a sweet relief ;
  Kneeling there in deep contrition,
  Help my unbelief.—*Cho.*

3 Trusting only in thy merit,
  Would I seek thy face ;
  Heal my wounded broken spirit,
  Save me by thy grace.—*Cho.*

4 Thou the spring of all my comfort,
  More than life to me ;
  Whom have I on earth beside thee?
  Whom in heaven but thee?—*Cho.*

Copyright, 1870, by W. H. DOANE. From "SONGS OF DEVOTION," by per. BIGLOW & MAIN.

255. TAPPAN. C. M.

ISAAC WATTS.   G. KINSLEY.

1 There is a land of pure delight,
  Where saints immortal reign ;
  ‖: Infinite day excludes the night, :‖
  And pleasures banish pain.

2 There everlasting spring abides,
  And never-withering flowers ;
  ‖: Death, like a narrow sea, divides :‖
  This heavenly land from ours.

3 Sweet fields beyond the swelling flood
  Stand dressed in living green ;
  ‖: So to the Jews old Canaan stood, :‖
  While Jordan rolled between.

4 But timorous mortals start and shrink
  To cross this narrow sea,
  ‖: And linger, shivering, on the brink, :‖
  And fear to launch away.

5 O could we make our doubts remove,
  Those gloomy doubts that rise,
  ‖: And see the Canaan that we love
  With unbeclouded eyes ;—

6 Could we but climb where Moses stood,
  And view the landscape o'er,
  ‖: Not Jordan's stream, nor death's cold flood, :‖
  Should fright us from the shore.

Songs for Home-Worship.

256. THE LORD WILL PROVIDE. 11, 6, 5.

Mrs. Martha Walker Cook.   Calvin Sears Harrington.

1 In some way or other the Lord will provide:
   It may not be my way,
   It may not be thy way,
   And yet, in his own way,
   "The Lord will provide."

2 At some time or other the Lord will provide:
   It may not be my time,
   It may not be thy time,
   And yet, in his own time,
   "The Lord will provide."

3 Despond then no longer, the Lord will provide:
   And this be the token,
   No word he hath spoken
   Was ever yet broken:
   "The Lord will provide."

4 March on, then, right boldly, the sea shall divide:
   The pathway made glorious,
   With shoutings victorious,
   We'll join in the chorus,
   "The Lord will provide."

257. RHINE. C. M.

Unknown.   F. Bergmuller.

1 Jerusalem, my happy home!
   Name ever dear to me!
   When shall my labors have an end
   ‖: In joy, and peace in thee? :‖

2 When shall these eyes thy heaven-built walls
   And pearly gates behold?
   Thy bulwarks with salvation strong,
   ‖: And streets of shining gold? :‖

3 There happier bowers than Eden's bloom,
   Nor sin nor sorrow know;
   Blest seats! thro' rude and stormy scenes
   ‖: I onward press to you. :‖

4 Apostles, martyrs, prophets, there
   Around my Saviour stand;
   And soon my friends in Christ below
   ‖: Will join the glorious band. :‖

5 Jerusalem, my happy home!
   My soul still pants for thee;
   Then shall my labors have an end,
   ‖: When I thy joys shall see. :‖

Songs for Home-Worship.

258. ST. JUDE. 6. D.

Rev. Benjamin Schmolke.
Carl Maria Von Weber.

1 My Jesus, as thou wilt:
O may thy will be mine;
Into thy hand of love
I would my all resign.
Thro' sorrow or through joy,
Conduct me as thine own,
And help me still to say,
My Lord, thy will be done.

2 My Jesus, as thou wilt:
If needy here and poor,
Give me thy people's bread,
Their portion rich and sure.
The manna of thy word
Let my soul feed upon;
And if all else should fail,
My Lord, thy will be done.

3 My Jesus, as thou wilt;
Tho' seen thro' many a tear,
Let not my star of hope
Grow dim or disappear.
Since thou on earth hast wept,
And sorrowed oft alone,
If I must weep with thee,
My Lord, thy will be done.

4 My Jesus, as thou wilt:
All shall be well for me;
Each changing future scene
I gladly trust with thee.
Straight to my home above,
I travel calmly on,
And sing in life or death,
My Lord, thy will be done.

259. LAST BEAM.

T. V. Weisenthal.

1 Fading, still fading, the last beam is shining:
Father in heaven! the day is declining,
Safety and innocence fly with the light,
Temptation and danger walk forth with the night;
From the fall of the shade till the morning bells chime,
Shield me from danger, save me from crime.
Ref.—Father, have mercy, Father have mercy,
Father, have mercy thro' Jesus Christ our Lord.

2 Father in heaven! O hear when we call,
Hear, for Christ's sake, who is Saviour of all;
Feeble and fainting we trust in thy might,
In doubting and darkness thy love be our light;
Let us sleep on thy breast while the night taper burns,
Wake in thy arms when morning returns.
Ref.—Father, have mercy, Father have mercy,
Father, have mercy thro' Jesus Christ our Lord.

Songs for Home-Worship.

260. I'M GOING HOME. L. M.

Rev. WM. HUNTER. William Miller.

1 My heavenly home is bright and fair;
Nor pain, nor death can enter there;
Its glittering towers the sun outshine;
That heavenly mansion shall be mine.

Cho.—I'm going home, I'm going home,
I'm going home to die no more,
To die no more, to die no more,
I'm going home to die no more.

2 My Father's house is built on high,
Far, far above the starry sky;
When from this earthly prison free,
That heavenly mansion mine shall be.—Cho.

3 While here a stranger far from home,
Affliction's waves may round me foam;
And, tho' like Lazarus, sick and poor,
My heavenly mansion is secure.—Cho.

4 Let others seek a home below,
Which flames devour, or waves o'erflow,
Be mine a happier lot to own,
A heavenly mansion near the throne.—Cho.

5 Then fail the earth, let stars decline,
And sun and moon refuse to shine,
All nature sick and cease to be,
That heavenly mansion stands for me.—Cho.

261. ALL TO CHRIST I OWE.

Mrs. ELVINA M. HALL. JOHN T. GRAPE, by per.

1 I hear the Saviour say,
Thy strength indeed is small,
Child of weakness, watch and pray,
Find in me thine all in all.

Cho.—Jesus paid it all,
All to him I owe;
Sin had left a crimson stain:
He washed it white as snow.

2 Lord, now indeed I find
Thy power, and thine alone,
Can change the leper's spots,
And melt the heart of stone.—Cho.

3 For nothing good have I
Whereby thy grace to claim—
I'll wash my garment white
In the blood of Calvary's Lamb.—Cho.

4 When from my dying bed
My ransomed soul shall rise,
Then "Jesus paid it all"
Shall rend the vaulted skies.—Cho.

5 And when before the throne
I stand in him complete,
I'll lay my trophies down,
All down at Jesus' feet.—Cho.

Songs for Home-Worship.

262. THE LORD'S PRAYER.

1. Our Father, who art in heaven, | hallowed | be thy | name ; ‖ thy kingdom come, thy will be done on | earth, . . as it | is in | heaven ;
2. Give us this | day our | daily | bread ; ‖ And forgive us our debts, as | we for- | give our | debtors.
3. And lead us not into temptation, but de- | liver | us from | evil ; ‖ For thine is the kingdom, and the power, and the glory, for- | ever. | A- | men.

263. EMMAUS. 11. 5.
Chant.   LODER.

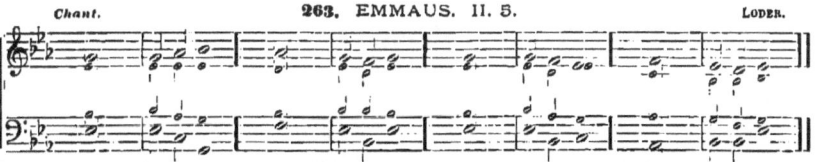

1 Abide with me! fast falls the | eventide,
The darkness deepens ; Lord, with | me abide :
When other helpers fail, and | comforts flee,
Help of the helpless, oh a- | bide with me.

2 Swift to its close ebbs out life's | little day :
Earth's joys grow dim, its glories | pass away ;
Change and decay on all a- | round I see ;
O thou who changest not, a- | bide with me.

3 I need thy presence every | passing hour ;
What but th grace can foil the | tempter's power?
Who like thyself, my guide and | stay can be ?
Thro' cloud and sunshine, Lord, a- | bide with me.

4 I fear no foe, with thee at | hand to bless ;
Ills have no weight, and tears no | bitterness.
Where is death's sting? where, grave, thy | victory?
I triumph still, if thou a- | bide with me.

5 Hold thou thy cross before my | closing eyes ;
Shine through the gloom, and point me | to the skies ;
Heaven's morning breaks, and earth's vain | shadows flee ;
In life, in death, O Lord, a- | bide with me.

JOHN BOWRING.

264. RATHBUN. 8. 7.
I. CONKEY.

1 In the cross of Christ I glory,
Towering o'er the wrecks of time ;
All the light of sacred story
Gathers round its head sublime.

2 When the woes of life o'ertake me,
Hopes deceive, and fears annoy,
Never shall the cross forsake me ;
Lo, it glows with peace and joy.

3 When the sun of bliss is beaming
Light and love upon my way,
From the cross the radiance streaming
Adds more lustre to the day.

4 Bane and blessing, pain and pleasure,
By the cross are sanctified ;
Peace is there, that knows no measure,
Joys that through all time abide.

Used by per. of O. DITSON & Co.

Songs for Home-Worship.

265. OLIPHANT. 8. 7. 4.
William Williams. — Arr. by L. Mason.

1 Guide me, O thou great Jehovah,
  Pilgrim through this barren land;
  I am weak, but thou art mighty,
  Hold me with thy powerful hand;
  ‖: Bread of heaven, :‖
  ‖: Feed me now and evermore. :‖

2 Open now the crystal fountain,
  Whence the healing streams do flow;
  Let the fiery, cloudy pillar
  Lead me all my journey through;
  ‖: Strong Deliverer, :‖
  ‖: Be thou still my strength and shield. :‖

3 When I tread the verge of Jordan,
  Bid my anxious fears subside,
  Death of death and hell's destruction,
  Land me safe on Canaan's side;
  ‖: Song of praises :‖
  ‖: I will ever give to thee.:‖

Used by per. of O. Ditson & Co.

266. SHINING SHORE. 8. 7. D
David Nelson. — Geo. F. Root.

REFRAIN.

1 My days are gliding swiftly by,
  And I, a pilgrim stranger,
  Would not detain them, as they fly,
  Those hours of toil and danger.

Ref.—For O, we stand on Jordan's strand;
  Our friends are passing over;
  And just before, the shining shore
  We may almost discover.

2 Our absent king the watchword gave,
  "Let every lamp be burning;"
  We look afar across the wave,
  Our distant home discerning.—Ref.

3 Should coming days be dark and cold,
  We will not yield to sorrow,
  For hope will sing, with courage bold,
  "There's glory on the morrow."—Ref.

4 Let storms of woe in whirlwinds rise,
  Each cord on earth to sever,
  There, bright and joyous in the skies,
  There, is our home forever.
  Ref.—For now we stand, etc.

Used by per. of O. Ditson & Co.

Songs for Home-Worship.

SARAH F. ADAMS. **267.** BETHANY. 6. 4. L. MASON.

1 Nearer, my God, to thee,
Nearer to thee!
E'en though it be a cross
That raiseth me,
Still all my song shall be,
||:Nearer, my God, to thee, :||
Nearer to thee!

2 Though like the wanderer,
The sun gone down,
Darkness be over me,
My rest a stone;
Yet in my dreams I'd be
||:Nearer, my God, to thee, :||
Nearer to thee!

3 There let the way appear
Steps unto heaven;
All that thou sendest me,
In mercy given;
Angels to beckon me
||:Nearer, my God, to thee, :||
Nearer to thee!

4 Then with my waking thoughts
Bright with thy praise,
Out of my stony griefs
Bethel I'll raise;
So by my woes to be
||:Nearer, my God, to thee, :||
Nearer to thee!

5 Or, if on joyful wing
Cleaving the sky,
Sun, moon, and stars forgot,
Upward I fly;
Still all my song shall be,
||:Nearer, my God, to thee, :||
Nearer to thee!

Used by per. of O. DITSON & Co.

GEO. COOPER. **268.** LET THE SAVIOUR IN. H. MILLARD.
Moderato.

1 Lo! he's knocking at every heart,—
Let the Saviour in!
Shall we tell him he must depart?—
Let the Saviour in!
He is waiting beside your door,
He is pleading forevermore!—
Your sweet welcome he doth implore,—
Let the Saviour in!

2 Would ye turn him in grief away?
Let the Saviour in!
Sister, brother, do not delay,—
Let the Saviour in!

He is mighty to save and keep,
He will comfort the eyes that weep!
In his presence how sweet our sleep!—
Let the Saviour in!

Take him fondly unto your breast,—
Let the Saviour in!
He will give to the weary rest,—
Let the Saviour in!
Shall his summons be heard in vain?
Shall we turn him away again?—
Ye who linger in doubt and pain,—
Let the Saviour in!

Copyright, 1872, by H. MILLARD.

Songs for Home-Worship.

269. GOD BLESS OUR HOME.

Con espress.   SICILIAN PASTORAL.

1 God bless our home forever,
   And all our loved ones there!
May no unkindness sever
   The hearts so true and fair!
O, may its light so loving
   Shine brightly 'mid the dark,
To lure from sin and roving
   Our sad, world-weary bark!

Cho.—Home, home; sweet, sweet home!
   God bless our home forever,
   Sweet heav'n is mirrored there

2 God bless our home where nightly
   We sing our songs of praise!
May joy be shining brightly
   Within it all our days!
Tho' death may seek to sever
   Our golden links of love,
O, may we meet forever
   In yonder home above!

Cho.—Home, home; sweet, sweet home!
   God bless our home forever,
   Sweet heav'n is mirrored there!

Copyright, 1872, by H. MILLARD.

270. WHAT A FRIEND WE HAVE IN JESUS.

ANON.   CHARLES C. CONVERSE, by per.

1.
What a friend we have in Jesus,
   All our sins and griefs to bear;
What a privilege to carry
   Every thing to God in prayer.
Oh, what peace we often forfeit,
   Oh, what needless pain we bear—
All because we do not carry
   Every thing to God in prayer.

2.
Have we trials and temptations?
   Is there trouble anywhere?
We should never be discouraged,
   Take it to the Lord in prayer.
Can we find a friend so faithful,
   Who will all our sorrows share?
Jesus knows our every weakness,
   Take it to the Lord in prayer.

3.
Are we weak and heavy laden,
   Cumbered with a load of care?
Precious Saviour, still our refuge,
   Take it to the Lord in prayer.
Do thy friends despise, forsake thee?
   Take it to the Lord in prayer;
In his arms he'll take and shield thee,
   Thou wilt find a solace there.

INDEX OF TUNES.

	PAGE
All to Christ I Owe	840
America	812
Antioch	792
Arlington	780
Armenia	782
Avon	792
Azmon	781
Baden	783
Be a Christian While You're Young	816
Beautiful Valley of Eden	834
Bethany	843
Blessed Homeland	836
Carroll	776
Chesterfield	777
Chimes	787
Christmas	813
Christmas Hymn	763
Colchester	770
Concord	764
Come, Brothers, Onward	814
Cowper	789
Dear Jesus	817
Dedham	794
Dennis	782
Denfield	799
Departing	787
Devizes	784
Ditchling	794
Dover	776
Downs	765
Emmaus	841
Evening Hymn	772
Every Day and Hour	832
Fane	802
Federal Street	770
Frederick II	836
Fuller	767
Geer	801
Gentle Words	826
Germany	763
God Bless Our Home	844

	PAGE
Groton	795
Guide us, Saviour	821
Happy Festal Day	821
Heber	828, 788
Hebron	771
He Leadeth Me	835
Hendon	806
Henry	793
Holbein	801
Holly	808
Home	785
Horton	809
Italian Hymn	813
I'm Going Home	840
I Need Thee Every Hour	829
Jesus Our Shepherd	822
Laban	791
Last Beam	839
Leaning	781
Let the Saviour In	843
Lisbon	796
London	805
Loving Kindness	785
Lowell	784
Lucerne	774
Mahaleth	799
Manoah	768
Marlow	795
Martyn	830
Mendon	811
Migdol	806
Morning Song	815
Morning Walks	826
Mornington	775
Montgomery	780
National	818
Naomi	791
Near the Cross	830
Nevermore be Sad or Weary	773
Newhope	779
Nineveh	804

Index of Tunes.

	PAGE		PAGE
Northfield	798	St. Jude	839
Nuremberg	810	St. Michael	777
		Stockwell	831
Oh! We are Volunteers	816	Stonefield	809
Old Hundred	810	St. Thomas	772
Olivet	832	"Suffer Little Children to Come Unto Me"	824
Oliphant	842	Sunday-School Festival Song	824
Olmutz	797	Sunday-School Volunteer Song	819
Olney	774	Swanwick	796
Ortonville	778	Sweet Hour of Prayer	812
Our Hearts are Young and Joyous	818		
Our Home Song	814	Tappan	837
Our Home with Jesus	822	Thatcher	788
Ova	797	Thaxted	800
		The Beautiful Land	823
Park Street	775	The Beautiful Way	826
Pass Me Not	837	The Gracious Choice	827
Pentonville	805	The Heavenly Land	825
Peterborough	778	The Hour of Prayer	815
Pleyel's Hymn	807	The Lord's Prayer	841
Portuguese Hymn	833	The Lord Will Provide	838
Praise the Giver of All	817	The Old, Old Story	831
		The Royal Proclamation	820
Rathburn	841	The Saviour's Love	819
Retreat	834	The Sweetest Name	828
Rhine	839	Truro	766
Rockingham	767		
Rock of Ages	812	Uxbridge	768
Rockville	800		
Rossini	793	Walton	803
Rothwell	764	Ward	769
		Warwick	769
Seasons	765	Warrington	770
Selvin	804	Webb	790
Seymour	773	Wells	807
Shining Shore	842	We Are Coming, Blessed Saviour	822
Shirland	786	"We Lift Our Tuneful Voices"	825
Silver Street	803	Welcome Hour of Prayer	813
Sing Hallelujah	827	West Point	802
Softly She Faded	815	What a Friend We Have in Jesus	844
Solney	811	What Can a Little Child Do?	823
Something for Jesus	833	Windham	786
Something to Do in Heaven	820	Winchester	780
Steele	808	Wirgman	798
Stephens	766	Woodstock	835
Stephanus	828	Woodworth	829
St. Gabriel	771		
St. John's	790	Zanesville	783

INDEX OF FIRST LINES.

A

	PAGE
Abide with me, fast falls the eventide	841
A broken heart—my God my king	786
A glory gilds the sacred page	793
A little child the Saviour came	811
All people that on earth do dwell	780
Amid the splendors of Thy state	801
A morning song to Thee we raise	815
Another six days' work is done	766
Arise ye people and adore	796
Arm of the Lord awake	810
Art thou weary, art thou languid	828
Asleep in Jesus, blessed sleep	780
Awake ! and sing the song	803
Awake from your slumber and come	826
Awake my soul, and with the sun	785
Awake my soul, stretch every nerve	778
Awake ye saints and raise your eyes	799

B

	PAGE
Beautiful valley of Eden	834
Beautiful way, hallowed and blest	826
Behold the glories of the Lamb	798
Behold the morning sun	804
Before Jehovah's awful throne	764
Blest are the pure in heart	782
Blest are the sons of peace	776
Blest hour when righteous souls shall meet	789
Bless, O my soul, the living God	763
Bright source of everlasting love	792

C

	PAGE
Cease ye mourners! cease to languish	773
Children of the heavenly King	763
Christ the Lord is risen to-day	806
Come, brothers, onward	814
Come, children, join to sing	827
Come, Holy Spirit, Heavenly Dove	766
Come in thou blessed of the Lord	798
Come let us join our cheerful songs	766
Come let us lift our joyful eyes	800
Come let us to the Lord our God	792
Come, Lord, and warm each languid heart	778
Come, O my soul ! in sacred lays	772
Come, said Jesus' sacred voice	809
Come sound His praise abroad	805
Come Thou Almighty King	813
Come we that love the Lord	802

D

	PAGE
Dear Father, to Thy mercy-seat	799
Dear Jesus ! ever at my side	817
Depth of Mercy !—can there be	808
Descend from heaven, immortal Dove !	764

E

	PAGE
Earth has a joy unknown in heaven	763
Early my God without delay	801
Eternal Wisdom, Thee we praise	797

F

	PAGE
Fading, still fading, the last beam	830
Faith adds new charms to earthly bliss	777
Faith to the conscience whispers peace	769
Far from these narrow scenes of night	767
Father of mercies, in Thy word	765
Fount of everlasting love !	763
From every stormy wind that blows	834

G

	PAGE
Gently, Lord, O gently lead us	811
Give to the winds thy fears	804
Gliding o'er life's fitful waters	836
Glory to the Father give	810
Glory to thee my God this night	772
God bless our home forever	844
God has said, forever blessed	821
God in the gospel of His Son	771
God moves in a mysterious way	783
God of my life! through all my days	770
Grace!—'tis a charming sound	805
Great Father of each perfect gift	791
Great God, we sing Thy mighty hand	776
Great God, how infinite art Thou	805
Great God, whose universal sway	809
Great is the Lord our God	783
Great God, to Thee my evening song	787
Guide me, O Thou great Jehovah	842

H

	PAGE
Happy, happy, festal eve	821
Happy the home when God is there	793

Index of First Lines.

	PAGE
Happy the man whose hopes rely	765
Happy the souls to Jesus joined	778
Hear the royal proclamation	820
He leadeth me, O blessed thought	835
High in the heavens eternal God	807
How beauteous are their feet	786
How blest the righteous when he dies	774
How blest the sacred tie that binds	786
How bright the glorious spirits shine	790
How charming is the place	775
How firm a foundation ye saints	833
How honored is the sacred place	788
How perfect is Thy word	772
How pleasant, how divinely fair	767
How shall the young secure their hearts	770
How sweet, how heavenly is the sight	778
How sweet the name of Jesus sounds	828
How swiftly the years have been rolling	818
How vain is all beneath the skies	774

I

I am weary of straying, Oh, fain would I	785
If through unruffled seas	782
I hear the Saviour say	840
I know that my Redeemer lives	802
I love Thy Kingdom, Lord	788
I love to steal awhile away	835
I love to think of the heavenly land	825
In all my vast concerns with Thee	805
I need Thee every hour	829
In some way or other the Lord will provide	838
In the cross of Christ I glory	841
I send the joys of earth away	787
I would not live alway	836

J

Jehovah, God! Thy gracious power	795
Jehovah reigns!—he dwells in light	780
Jerusalem, my happy home	836
Jesus is our Shepherd, wiping every tear	822
Jesus keep me near the cross	830
Jesus, lover of my soul	830
Jesus my all to heaven is gone	781
Jesus shall reign where'er the sun	775
Jesus, who knows full well	797
Joy to the world, the Lord is come	792
Just as I am, without one plea	829

L

Let children hear the mighty deeds	784
Let every mortal ear attend	803
Let saints below in concert sing	804
Let us mingle our voices in chorus to-day	817
Lift up your heads, eternal gates	782
Like sheep we went astray	791

	PAGE
Lo! He's knocking at every heart	843
Long as I live I'll bless Thy name	794
Lord, at Thy table I behold	787
Lord, in the morning Thou shalt hear	783
Lord, we come before Thee now	809
Lord, when we bend before Thy throne	801

M

Majestic sweetness sits enthroned	781
Mid scenes of confusion and creature	785
Might I enjoy the meanest place	765
Morning breaks upon the tomb	807
My country 'tis of thee	812
My days are gliding swiftly by	812
My dear Redeemer and my Lord	808
My faith looks up to Thee	832
My God, my Life, my Love	803
My Sun, my Portion, and my Love	799
My God, the spring of all my joys	804
My God, Thy service well demands	769
My heavenly home is bright and fair	840, 822
My Jesus, as Thou wilt	839
My Saviour, my Almighty Friend	797
My soul, be on thy guard	796
My soul, it is thy God	772
My soul, repeat His praise	776
My spirit, on thy care	774, 796

N

Nearer my God to Thee	843
New every morning is the love	810
No change of time shall ever shock	811
No more, my God, I boast no more	781
Now let our souls on wings sublime	784
Now the shades of night are gone	773

O

O, all ye lands, rejoice in God	792
O, cease my wandering soul	788
O God, beneath Thy guiding hand	766
O God, my heart is fully bent	793
Oh for a closer walk with God	769
Oh for a faith that will not shrink	777
Oh for a heart to praise my God	770
Oh for the peace of those	802
Oh for a shout of sacred joy	800
Oh happy is the man that hears	801
Oh praise the Lord for he is good	795
Oh 'twas a joyful sound to hear	799
Oh won't you be a Christian while	816
Oh we are volunteers in the army of the Lord	816
O Lord, how full of sweet content	808
O Lord our God, arise	764
O Lord, Thy heavenly grace impart	768
Once more my soul the rising day	803

Index of First Lines.

	PAGE
One sweetly solemn thought	775
On Jordan's stormy banks I stand	767
O Thou from whom all goodness flows	780
Our Father who art in heaven	841
Our Heavenly Father hear	791
Our hearts are very joyful	814
Our hearts are young and joyous	818

P

Pass me not, O gentle Saviour	837
Praise, Lord, for Thee in Zion waits	770
Praise the Lord, His glories show	798
Praise to Him whose love has given	907
Praise to the radiant source of bliss	793

R

Remember thy Creator now	794
Return, O wanderer! now return	791
Rock of Ages, cleft for me	812

S

Saviour, may a little child	814
Saviour, more than life to me	832
Saviour, source of every blessing	831
Saviour, Thy dying love	833
See the heathen nations bending	790
See! Jesus stands with open arms	768
Since all the varying scenes of time	795
Soft be the gentle breathing notes	819
Softly fades the twilight ray	807
Softly now the light of day	798
Softly she faded as fades the twilight	815
So let our lips and lives express	785
Songs of praise the angels sang	806
Still with Thee, O my God	788
Sun of my soul, thou Saviour dear	771
Sweet hour of prayer	812
Sweet is the memory of thy grace	790
Sweet is the work my God, my King	775

T

Tarry with me, O my Saviour	811
Tell me the old, old story	831
Thee we adore, eternal Lord	768
The heavens declare thy glory, Lord	767
The Lord is risen indeed	764
The Lord, how wondrous are His ways	806
The morning light is breaking	790
The spacious firmament on high	770
There's a beautiful land where flowers	823
There is a fold whence none can stray	768
There is a glorious world of light	780
There is an eye that never sleeps	788

	PAGE
There is a land of pure delight	794, 837
There'll be something in heaven for children to do	820
There is no name so sweet on earth	828
The sun may warm the grass to life	826
Thine earthly Sabbaths, Lord, we love	806
Thine forever, Lord of life	810
This is not my place of resting	773
This is the day the Lord hath made	789
Thou art the way, to Thee alone	781
Thou must go forth alone, my soul	794
Through endless years Thou art the same	800
Through every age, eternal God	809
Thus far the Lord hath led me on	771
'Tis by Thy strength the mountains stood	800
To God the only wise	707
To our Redeemer's glorious name	787
To Thy pastures fair and large	773

U

Up to the hills I lift mine eyes	776

W

We are coming, blessed Saviour	822
We are marching on with shield and banner bright	819
We are on the ocean sailing	827
We gather once more in our pleasant retreat	824
We lift our tuneful voices now	825
Welcome sweet day of rest	786
We've no abiding city here	780
What a friend we have in Jesus	844
What can a little child like me	823
What did our Lord and Saviour say	824
What shall I render to my God	777
What though downy slumbers flee	809
When all thy mercies, O my God	802
When God revealed His gracious name	777
When I survey the wondrous cross	770
When morning dawns with glorious light	815
When softly o'er the distant hills	813
When the worn spirit wants repose	779
When we in darkness walk	774
While shepherds watched their flocks by night	813
Whilst Thee I seek, protecting power	779
Why should the children of a King	765
Why should we start and fear to die	771
With joy we hail the sacred day	782
With joy we meditate the grace	784
With tearful eyes we look around	769
Witness ye men and angels now	796

Y

Ye nations round the earth rejoice	784
Ye hosts of heaven, ye mighty ones	795

www.ingramcontent.com/pod-product-compliance
Lightning Source LLC
Chambersburg PA
CBHW020258090426
42735CB00009B/1138